# Windows® 8

FOR

# DUMMIES®

POCKET EDITION

## by Andy Rathbone

WILEY

John Wiley & Sons, Inc.

# Windows® 8 For Dummies® Pocket Edition

Published by
**John Wiley & Sons, Inc.**
111 River Street
Hoboken, NJ 07030-5774

www.wiley.com

Copyright © 2012 by John Wiley & Sons, Inc., Hoboken, New Jersey

Published by John Wiley & Sons, Inc., Hoboken, New Jersey

Published simultaneously in Canada

For general information on our other products and services, please contact our Customer Care Department within the U.S. at 877-762-2974, outside the U.S. at 317-572-3993, or fax 317-572-4002.

For technical support, please visit www.wiley.com/techsupport.

Wiley publishes in a variety of print and electronic formats and by print-on-demand. Some material included with standard print versions of this book may not be included in e-books or in print-on-demand. If this book refers to media such as a CD or DVD that is not included in the version you purchased, you may download this material at http://booksupport.wiley.com. For more information about Wiley products, visit www.wiley.com.

ISBN 978-1-118-37166-4 (ppk); ISBN 978-1-118-51355-2 (ebk); ISBN 978-1-118-51360-6 (ebk); ISBN 978-1-118-51357-6 (ebk)

Manufactured in the United States of America

10 9 8 7 6 5 4 3 2 1

WILEY

# About the Author

**Andy Rathbone** started geeking around with computers in 1985 when he bought a 26-pound portable CP/M Kaypro 2X. Like other nerds of the day, he soon began playing with null-modem adapters, dialing computer bulletin boards, and working part-time at Radio Shack.

He wrote articles for various techie publications before moving to computer books in 1992. He's written the *Windows For Dummies* series, *Upgrading and Fixing PCs For Dummies*, *TiVo For Dummies*, *PCs: The Missing Manual*, and many other computer books.

Today, he has more than 15 million copies of his books in print, and they've been translated into more than 30 languages. You can reach Andy at his website, www.andyrathbone.com.

# Author's Acknowledgments

Special thanks to Dan Gookin, Matt Wagner, Tina Rathbone, Steve Hayes, Nicole Sholly, Virginia Sanders, and Russ Mullen.

Thanks also to all the folks I never meet in editorial, sales, marketing, proofreading, layout, graphics, and manufacturing who work hard to bring you this book.

# Publisher's Acknowledgments

We're proud of this book; please send us your comments at
http://dummies.custhelp.com. For other comments, please contact
our Customer Care Department within the U.S. at 877-762-2974, outside
the U.S. at 317-572-3993, or fax 317-572-4002.

Some of the people who helped bring this book to market include the
following:

*Acquisitions and Editorial*

**Sr. Project Editor:** Nicole Sholly

**Executive Editor:** Steven Hayes

**Copy Editor:** Virginia Sanders

**Technical Editor:** Russ Mullen

**Editorial Manager:** Jodi Jensen

**Editorial Assistant:**
Leslie Saxman

**Sr. Editorial Assistant:**
Cherie Case

**Cover Photo:** © imagewerks/
Getty Images

*Composition Services*

**Project Coordinator:**
Sheree Montgomery

**Layout and Graphics:** Carl Byers,
Carrie A. Cesavice,
Tim Detrick

**Proofreader:** John Greenough

**Publishing and Editorial for Technology Dummies**

    **Richard Swadley,** Vice President and Executive Group Publisher

    **Andy Cummings,** Vice President and Publisher

    **Mary Bednarek,** Executive Acquisitions Director

    **Mary C. Corder,** Editorial Director

**Publishing for Consumer Dummies**

    **Kathleen Nebenhaus,** Vice President and Executive Publisher

**Composition Services**

    **Debbie Stailey,** Director of Composition Services

# Table of Contents

# Introduction

● ● ● ● ● ● ● ● ● ● ● ● ● ● ● ● ● ● ● ● ● ● ● ● ● ● ● ● ● ● ● ●

*T*his Pocket Edition isn't intended to make you a whiz at Windows; instead, it dishes out chunks of useful computing information when you need them. You don't have to become a Windows 8 expert, you just need to know enough to get by quickly, cleanly, and with a minimum of pain so that you can move on to the more pleasant things in life.

Best of all, you can get what you need out of this book whether you're working on a touchscreen, laptop, or desktop computer.

## About This Book

Treat this book like you would a dictionary or other reference text. Turn to the page with the information you need and say, "Ah, so that's what they're talking about." Then put down the book and move on.

Instead of fancy computer jargon, this book covers the topics you're looking for in plain English. You don't have to memorize anything. Just turn to the appropriate page, read the brief explanation, and get back to work. Unlike other books, this one enables you to bypass the technical hoopla and still get your work done.

# How to Use This Book

When something in Windows 8 leaves you stumped, find the troublesome topic in this book's table of contents or index, turn to what you need, and then apply what you've read.

If you have to type something into the computer, you'll see easy-to-follow bold text like this:

Type **Media Player** into the Search box.

When I describe a key combination you should press, I describe it like this:

Press Ctrl+B.

This means to hold down your keyboard's Control key while pressing your keyboard's B key. Whenever I present a website address, I show it this way: www. andyrathbone.com.

# Tablet Owners Aren't Left Out

Although Windows 8 comes preinstalled on all new Windows computers, Microsoft not-so-secretly aims this bold new version of Windows at owners of *touch-screens.* Tablets, as well as some laptops and desktop monitors, come with screens you can control by touching them with your fingers.

If you're a new touchscreen owner, don't worry. This book explains where you need to touch, slide, or tap your finger in all the appropriate places. If you find yourself scratching your head over explanations aimed at mouse owners, remember these three touch-screen rules:

✔ **When told to *click*, you should *tap*.** Quickly touching and releasing your finger on a button is the same as clicking it with a mouse.

✔ **When told to double-click, *tap twice*.** Two touches in rapid succession does the trick.

✔ **When told to *right-click* something, *hold down your finger on the item*. Then, when a little menu pops up, *lift your finger*.** The menu stays put onscreen. (That's exactly what would have happened if you'd right-clicked the item with a mouse.) While you're looking at the pop-up menu, tap any of its listed items to have Windows carry out your bidding.

If you find touchscreens to be cumbersome while you're sitting at a desk, you can always plug a mouse and keyboard into your touch-screen tablet. They'll work just fine. In fact, they usually work better when working on the Windows desktop rather than the Start screen.

# Icons Used in This Book

It just takes a glance at Windows 8 to notice its *icons*, which are little push-button pictures for starting various programs. The icons in this book fit right in, and they're even a little easier to figure out.

Watch out! This signpost warns you that technical information is coming around the bend.

This icon alerts you about juicy information that makes computing easier: a method for keeping the cat from sleeping on top of your tablet, for example.

Don't forget to remember these important points. (Or at least dog-ear the pages so that you can look them up later.)

 The computer won't explode while you're performing the delicate operations associated with this icon. Still, wearing gloves and proceeding with caution is a good idea.

 Are you moving to Windows 8 from an older Windows version? This icon alerts you to areas where Windows 8 works significantly differently from its predecessors.

 Controlled by your fingertip rather than a mouse and keyboard, a touchscreen is standard fare on tablets, as well as some newer laptops and desktop monitors. This icon appears next to information aimed directly at the touchy feely crowd.

## *Where to Go from Here*

Now, you're ready for action. Give the pages a quick flip and scan a section or two that you know you'll need later. Please remember, this is *your* book — your weapon against the computer nerds who've inflicted this whole complicated computer concept on you. Please circle any paragraphs you find useful, highlight key concepts, add your own sticky notes, and doodle in the margins next to the complicated stuff.

To access additional Windows 8 content, go to www. dummies.com/go/windows8. Occasionally, we have updates to our technology books. If this book does have technical updates, they will be posted at www. dummies.com/go/windows8fdupdates.

# Chapter 1

# The New Start Screen

- - - - - - - - - - - - - - - - - - - - - - - - - - - - - -

### In This Chapter

▶ Finding out what's new in Windows 8

▶ Signing in to Windows 8

▶ Understanding the Start screen

▶ Getting used to the Charms bar

▶ Checking out the free apps

▶ Getting out of Windows 8

- - - - - - - - - - - - - - - - - - - - - - - - - - - - - -

*W*indows 8 definitely changes up your Windows experience. It still comes with the traditional Windows desktop, but the new Start screen is creating all the excitement. The Start screen's large, colorful tiles offer quick stepping stones for checking e-mail, watching videos, and sampling Internet fare.

## What's New in Windows 8?

If you've worked with earlier versions of Microsoft Windows, get ready to toss away much of that hard-earned knowledge. Windows 8 essentially starts from scratch in an attempt to please two camps of computer owners.

Some people are mostly *consumers.* They read e-mail, watch videos, listen to music, and browse the web, often while away from their desktop PC. Whether on the go or on the couch, they're consuming media (and popcorn).

Other people are mostly *creators.* They write papers, prepare tax returns, update blogs, edit videos, or, quite often, tap whichever keys their boss requires that day.

To please both markets, Microsoft broke Windows 8 into two very different modes:

✔ **Start screen:** For the on-the-go information grabbers, the Windows 8 Start screen fills the entire screen with large, colorful tiles that constantly update to show the latest stock prices, weather, e-mail, Facebook updates, and other tidbits. That information now appears before you touch a button. And *touch* is the keyword here: The Start screen is designed for *touchscreens* — those screens controlled with your fingertip. But the Start screen now also appears on your desktop PC, not just on your phone or tablet computer (see Figure 1-1). Be prepared for some initial mouse awkwardness as you try to mimic a fingertip with your mouse pointer.

✔ **Desktop tile:** When it's time for work, head for the Start screen's *desktop* tile. The traditional Windows desktop appears, shown in Figure 1-2, bringing all its power — as well as its detailed, cumbersome menus.

**Figure 1-1:** The newest version of Windows, Windows 8, comes preinstalled on most new PCs today.

**Figure 1-2:** The Windows 8 desktop works much as it did in Windows 7, but without a Start button.

In a way, Windows 8 offers the best of both worlds: You can stay on the Start screen for quick, on-the-go browsing. And when work beckons, you can head for the desktop, where your traditional Windows programs await.

Because the Windows desktop no longer contains the traditional Start button and Start menu that sprouted from the corner, you now must retreat to the new Start *screen.* To open a program, click or tap a program's tile from the Start screen, and Windows shuffles you back to the desktop, where the newly opened program awaits.

Love it or hate it, the new Start screen plays an integral role in Windows 8. This chapter explains how to make the most of it, whether you want to enjoy it or avoid it as much as possible. You find out more about the desktop in Chapter 2.

If you find yourself staring glumly at the confusing new Start screen, try these tricks: Right-click a blank spot, or point at any screen corner with your mouse. Those actions fetch hidden menus, bringing you a glimmer of navigational hope.

If you're using a touchscreen computer, substitute the word *tap* when you read the word *click.* Tapping twice works like *double-clicking.* And when you see the term *right-click,* touch and hold your finger on the glass; lift your finger when the right-click menu appears.

## Starting Windows 8

Starting Windows 8 is as easy as turning on your computer — Windows 8 leaps onto the screen automatically with a flourish. But before you can begin working, Windows 8 stops you cold: It displays a locked screen, shown in Figure 1-3, with no entrance key dangling nearby.

**Figure 1-3:** To move past this lock screen, drag up on the screen with your mouse or finger, or press a key on the keyboard.

Previous versions of Windows let you sign in as soon as you turned on your computer. Windows 8, by contrast, makes you unlock a screen before moving to the sign in page, where you type in your name and password.

How you unlock the lock screen depends on whether you're using a mouse, keyboard, or touchscreen:

- ✓ **Mouse:** On a desktop PC or laptop, click any mouse button.

- ✓ **Keyboard:** Press any key, and the lock screen slides away. Easy!

- ✓ **Touch:** Touch the screen with your finger and then slide your finger *up* the glass. A quick flick of the finger will do.

When you're in the door, Windows wants you to *sign in,* as shown in Figure 1-4, by clicking your name and typing in a password.

**Figure 1-4:** Click your user account name and then type your name and password on the next screen.

I've customized my Sign In screen. Yours will look different. If you don't see an account listed for you on the Sign In screen, you have several options:

- ✔ **If you see your name and e-mail address listed, type your password.** Windows 8 lets you in and displays your Start screen, just as you last left it.

- ✔ **If you don't see your name, but you have an account on the computer, click the left-pointing arrow.** Windows 8 displays a list of *all* the account holders. You may see the computer owner's name, as well as an account for Administrator and one for Guest.

✔ **If you just bought the computer, use the account named Administrator.** Designed to give the owner full power over the computer, the Administrator account user can set up new accounts for other people, install programs, start an Internet connection, and access *all* the files on the computer — even those belonging to other people. Windows 8 needs at least one person to act as administrator.

✔ **Use the Guest account.** Designed for household visitors, this account lets guests, such as the babysitter or visiting relatives, use the computer temporarily.

✔ **No Guest account?** Then find out who owns the computer and beg that person to set up an account for you or to turn on the Guest account.

Don't *want* to sign in at the Sign In screen? The screen's two bottom-corner buttons offer these other options:

✔ **The little wheelchair-shaped button in the screen's bottom-left corner,** shown in Figure 1-4 and the margin, customizes Windows 8 for people with physical challenges in hearing, sight, or manual dexterity. If you choose this button by mistake, click or touch on a different part of the screen to avoid changing any settings.

✔ **The little button in the screen's bottom-right corner,** shown in Figure 1-4 and the margin, lets you shut down or restart your PC. (If you've accidentally clicked it and shut down your PC, don't panic. Press your PC's power button, and your PC will return to this screen.)

Even while locked, as shown in Figure 1-3, your computer's screen displays current information in its bottom-left corner. Depending on how it's configured, you can see the time and date; your wireless Internet signal strength (the more bars, the better); battery strength (the more colorful the icon, the better); your next scheduled appointment; a count of unread e-mail; and other items.

## *Keeping your account private with a password*

Because Windows 8 lets many people use the same computer, how do you stop Rob from reading Diane's love letters to Jason Bieber? How can Josh keep Grace from deleting his *Star Wars* movie trailers? Using a *password* solves some of those problems.

In fact, a password is more important than ever in Windows 8 because some accounts can be tied to a credit card. By typing a secret password when signing in, as shown in Figure 1-5, you enable your computer to recognize *you* and nobody else. If you protect your username with a password, nobody can access your files. And nobody can rack up charges for computer games while you're away from home.

To set up or change your password, follow these steps:

1. **Summon the Charms bar and click the Settings icon.**

   You fetch the Charms bar differently depending on whether you're using a mouse, keyboard, or touchscreen:

   • *Mouse:* Move the mouse pointer to the top-right or bottom-right corner of your screen.

- *Keyboard:* Hold down the  key and press the letter C.

- *Touchscreens:* Slide your finger from the screen's right edge inward.

When the Charms bar appears, click the Settings icon. The Settings screen appears.

2. **Click the words Change PC Settings at the very bottom of the Settings screen.**

   The PC Settings screen appears.

3. **Click the Users category on the left and then click the Change Your Password button. Or, to create a password, click the Create a Password button.**

   You may need to type your existing password to gain entrance.

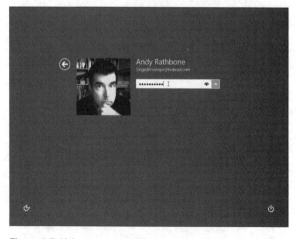

**Figure 1-5:** Using a password keeps your private material private.

4. **Type a password that will be easy to remember.**

 Choose something like the name of your favorite vegetable, for example, or your dental floss brand. To beef up its security level, capitalize some letters and embed a number in the password, like **Glide2** or **Ask4More**. (Don't use these exact two examples, though, because they've probably been added to every password cracker's arsenal by now.)

5. **If asked, type that same password into the Retype Password box, so Windows knows you're spelling it correctly.**

6. **In the Password Hint box, type a hint that reminds you — and only you — of your password.**

   Windows won't let you type in your exact password as a hint. You have to be a bit more creative.

7. **Click the Next button, and click Finish.**

   Suspect you've botched something during this process? Click Cancel to return to Step 3 and either start over or exit.

After you've created the password, Windows 8 begins asking for your password whenever you sign in.

   ✔ Passwords are *case-sensitive.* The words *Caviar* and *caviar* are considered two different passwords.

   ✔ Windows also offers to Create a Picture Password in Step 3, where you drag a finger or mouse over a photo in a certain sequence. Then, instead of entering a password, you redraw that sequence on the sign-in picture. (Picture passwords work much better on touchscreen tablets than desktop monitors.)

✔ Another new option in Step 3 is Create a PIN. A *PIN* is a four-digit code like the ones punched into Automated Teller Machines (ATMs). The disadvantage of a PIN? There's no password hint to a four-digit password.

## Signing up for a Microsoft account

Whether you're signing in to Windows 8 for the first time, trying to access some Start screen apps, or just trying to change a setting, you'll eventually see a screen similar to the one in Figure 1-6.

**Figure 1-6:** You need a Microsoft account to access many of the Windows 8 features.

That screen appears because Windows 8 introduces a new type of user account. You can sign in with either a *Microsoft* account or a *Local* account. Each serves a different need:

✔ **Microsoft account:** Consisting of an e-mail address and a password, this lets you download apps from the Windows Store and run all the bundled apps in Windows 8. You can link a Microsoft account with your social media accounts, automatically stocking your address book with your friends from Facebook, Twitter, and other sites. (Plus, you can access both your own and your friends' Facebook photos.)

✔ **Local account:** This account works fine for people working with traditional Windows programs on the Windows desktop. Local account holders can't run many of the Start screen apps bundled with Windows 8, including the Mail app. Nor can they download new apps from the Windows Store.

You have two ways to sign in with a Microsoft account; they're ranked here according to simplicity:

✔ **Use an existing Microsoft account.** If you already use Hotmail, Xbox Live, or Windows Messenger, you already have a Microsoft account and password. Type in that e-mail address and password at the screen shown in Figure 1-6 and then click the Sign In button.

✔ **Sign up for a new Microsoft account.** Click the Sign Up for a Microsoft Account link, shown in Figure 1-6, and Microsoft takes you to a website where you can turn your existing e-mail address into a Microsoft account. (Signing up for a new Microsoft e-mail address is a better option, however, because it lets you use the Windows 8 built-in Mail app.)

If you're signing into Windows 8 for the first time, and you don't want a Microsoft account, you'll see a Cancel button. Click Cancel, and the next screen shows a button that lets you sign in with a Local account instead.

But until you create a Microsoft account, the nag screen in Figure 1-6 will haunt you whenever you try to access a Windows 8 feature that requires a Microsoft account.

# *Figuring Out the New Start Screen in Windows 8*

The new Start screen in Windows 8 whisks you away from the traditional Windows desktop and drops you into a foreign land with no helpful translator at your side. That's right: Windows 8 no longer has a Start button *or* a Start menu.

Instead, the new Windows 8 Start *screen,* shown in Figure 1-7, appears whenever you turn on your computer. Whereas older Windows versions had a small Start menu on a desktop, the Windows 8 Start screen fills the entire screen with large tiles stretching beyond the right edge. Each tile represents a program installed on your computer.

**Figure 1-7:** Click a Start screen tile to start a program.

As you work, you'll constantly switch between the screen-filling Start screen and the traditional screen-filling desktop, covered in the next chapter.

Despite the drastic remodel, the Start screen still offers a way to start programs; adjust Windows settings; find help for sticky situations; or, thankfully, shut down Windows and get away from the computer for a while. Some Start screen tiles needn't be opened to see their contents. For example, the Calendar tile constantly updates to show the current date and day, as well as your next few appointments. The Mail tile cycles through the first words of your latest e-mails.

Your Start screen will change as you add more programs and apps to your computer. That's why the Start screen on your friend's computer, as well as in this book, is probably arranged differently than your computer's Start screen.

Try the following tricks to make the Start screen feel a little more like home:

- ✔ See the Start screen's tile named Desktop? Click that one to fetch the familiar Windows desktop. Whew! If you prefer to avoid the Start screen, you can stay on the traditional Windows desktop as much as possible. (I explain the desktop in Chapter 2.)

- ✔ Does your mouse have a little wheel embedded in its back? Spin the wheel, and the Start screen moves to the left or right, accordingly. It's a handy way to move quickly across the entire Start screen, from left to right.

- ✔ As you move your mouse pointer, the Start screen follows along. When the pointer reaches the screen's right edge, for example, the Start screen brings the offscreen portions into view.

> ✔ See the little bar along the Start screen's bottom edge? That's a *scroll bar*. Drag the scroll bar's light-colored portion to the left or right: As you move that portion, the Start screen moves along with it, letting you see items living off the screen's right edge.

> ✔ On a touchscreen, navigate the Start screen with your finger: Pretend the Start screen is a piece of paper lying on a table. As you move your finger, the Start screen moves along with it.

> ✔ On a keyboard, press the right- or left-arrow keys, and the Start screen's tiles move accordingly. Press the keyboard's End key to move to the end of the Start screen; the Home key moves you back to the Start screen's front.

## Launching a Start screen program or app

Windows 8 stocks your Start screen with *apps* — small programs for performing simple tasks. In fact, Windows 8 now refers to *all* Windows programs as apps. (It even refers to your once almighty desktop as the *Desktop app*.)

Each tile on the Start screen is a button for starting an app or traditional Windows program. Click the button, and the program or app jumps into action. Windows 8 complicates matters, as it offers several ways to push a button:

> ✔ **Mouse:** Point at the tile and click the left mouse button.

> ✔ **Keyboard:** Press the arrow keys until a box surrounds the desired tile. Then press the Enter key.

> ✔ **Touchscreens:** Tap the tile with your finger.

No matter which item you've chosen, it fills the screen, ready to inform you, entertain you, or maybe even do both. I explain the Start screen's built-in apps later in this chapter. If you feel like digging in, you can begin downloading and installing your own by clicking the Start screen's Store tile. (I explain how to download apps in Chapter 4.)

## Viewing or closing your open apps

Start screen apps, by nature, consume the entire screen, with no visible menus. That makes it difficult not only to control them but also to switch among them. The same holds true when you're working in the separate world of the traditional Windows desktop.

How do you switch between recently used programs and apps? Windows 8 makes it fairly easy to switch between them by following these steps:

1. **Point the mouse pointer at the screen's bottom-most-left corner.**

   A thumbnail of your last used app appears. You can click to bring that app to the screen. Or, if you want to revisit other apps running in the background, move to the next step.

2. **When the desktop icon appears, raise your mouse pointer along the screen's left edge.**

   As you move it up the screen, shown in Figure 1-8, a bar appears alongside the screen's left edge, showing thumbnails of your open apps.

To switch to any recently used app, click its thumbnail.

To see your last-used app, point in this corner; when the app's thumbnail appears, click it to switch to the app.

To see other recently used apps, point in the bottom-left corner. Then slide your mouse up the screen's left edge, and these thumbnails of your recently used apps appear.

**Figure 1-8:** Point in the bottom-left corner of the Start screen. Slide your mouse up the edge to see a list of currently running Start screen apps.

3. **To return to an app, click its thumbnail.**

4. **To close an app, right-click its thumbnail and choose Close.**

These tips can help you keep track of your running apps, as well as close down the ones you no longer want open:

✔ To cycle through your currently running apps, hold down the ▦ key and press Tab. The same bar you see in Figure 1-8 appears along the left edge. Each time you press Tab, you select another app. When you select the app you want, let go of the ▦ key, and the app fills the screen.

✔ You can view your most-recently-used apps whether you're working on the Windows desktop or on the new Start screen. From the desktop, point your mouse at the screen's bottom-left corner, slide the mouse up the screen's left edge, and then click the app you want to revisit.

✔ After you close an app in Step 4, the bar listing your running apps stays onscreen. You can then close other apps by right-clicking them and choosing Close, as well.

✔ To close an app you're currently working on, point your mouse at the screen's top edge. When the mouse pointer turns into a hand, hold down your mouse button and drag the app toward the screen's bottom. When your mouse reaches the screen's bottom edge, you've closed the app. (This trick works on the desktop, as well.)

## Finding a Start screen app or program

You can scroll through the Start screen until your eagle-eyes spot the tile you need, and then you can pounce on it with a quick mouse click or finger tap. But when the thrill of the hunt wanes, Windows 8 offers several shortcuts for finding apps and programs hidden inside a tile-stuffed Start screen.

When searching for a particularly elusive app or program, try these tricks:

✔ Mouse users can right-click on a blank portion of the Start screen. A bar rises from the screen's bottom showing an icon named All Apps (shown in the margin). Click the All Apps icon to see an alphabetical listing of *all* your computer's apps and programs. Click the desired app or program to open it.

✔ While looking at the Start screen, keyboard owners can simply begin typing the name of their desired app or program, like this: **face-book**. As you type, Windows 8 lists all the apps matching what you've typed so far, eventually narrowing down the search to the runaway.

✔ On a touchscreen, slide your finger up from the screen's bottom. When the bottom menu appears, tap the All Apps icon to see an alphabetical list of all your apps and programs.

## *Adding or removing Start screen items*

Removing something from the Start screen is easy, so you can begin there. To remove an unwanted or unused tile from the Start screen, right-click it and choose Unpin from Start from the pop-up menu along the screen's bottom. The unloved tile slides away without fuss.

But you'll probably want to spend more time *adding* items to the Start screen, and here's why: It's easy to escape the Start screen by clicking the Desktop app. But once you're safely on the desktop, how do you start a program without heading back to the Start screen? To escape this recursive conundrum, stock your Start screen with icons for your favorite desktop destinations, such as programs, folders, and settings. Then, instead of loading the desktop and looking lost, you can head to your final destination straight from the Start screen.

To add programs or apps to the Start screen, follow these steps:

1. **Press the Start screen's All Apps button.**

   Right-click a blank portion of the Start screen (or press ▓+Z) and then choose the All Apps button along the screen's bottom.

   On a touchscreen, slide your finger upward from the screen's bottom edge and then tap the All Apps icon.

   No matter which route you take, the Start screen alphabetically lists all your installed apps and programs.

2. **Right-click the item you want to appear on the Start screen and choose Pin to Start.**

3. **Repeat Step 2 for every item you want to add.**

   Unfortunately, you can't select and add several items simultaneously.

4. **Choose the Desktop app.**

   The desktop appears.

5. **Right-click desired items and choose Pin to Start.**

   Right-click a library, folder, file, or other item you want added to the Start screen; when the pop-up menu appears, choose Pin to Start.

When you're through, your Start screen will have grown considerably with all your newly added destinations.

## *The Charms bar and its shortcuts*

The Charms bar is simply a menu, one of a million in Windows 8. But the Microsoft marketing department, eager to impart a little humanity to your computer, calls it a *Charms bar*.

Shown in Figure 1-9, the Charms bar's five icons, or *charms,* list things you can do with your currently viewed screen. For example, when you're gazing at a website you want a friend to see, fetch the Charms bar, choose Share, and choose the friend who should see it. Off it goes to your friend's eyeballs.

**Figure 1-9:** The Charms bar in Windows 8 contains handy icons for performing common tasks.

The Charms bar can be summoned from *anywhere* within Windows 8, whether you're on the Start screen, the Windows desktop, and even from within apps and desktop programs.

But no matter what part of Windows 8 you're working with, you can summon the Charms bar using a mouse, keyboard, or touchscreen by following these steps:

> ✔ **Mouse:** Point at the top- or bottom-right corner.
>
> ✔ **Keyboard:** Press ⊞+C.
>
> ✔ **Touchscreen:** Slide your finger inward from the screen's right edge.

When the Charms bar appears, lingering along your screen's right edge, it sports five icons, ready to be either clicked or touched. Here's what each icon does:

✔ **Search:** Choose this, and Windows assumes you want to search through what you're currently seeing onscreen. To expand your search, choose one of the other search locations: Apps, Settings, or Files.

✔ **Share:** This fetches options for sharing what's currently on your screen. When viewing a web page, for example, a click of the Share button lets you choose Mail to e-mail the page's link to a friend. (I cover e-mail in Chapter 5.)

✔ **Start:** This simply takes you back to the Start screen. The ⊞ key on your keyboard or tablet also whisks you back there.

✔ **Devices:** Choose this to send your current screen's information to another device, such as a printer, second monitor, or perhaps a phone. (The Devices option lists only devices that are currently connected with your computer and able to receive the screen's information.)

✔ **Settings:** This lets you quickly tweak your computer's six major settings: Wi-Fi/Network, Volume, Screen, Notifications, Power, and Keyboard/Language. Not enough? Then choose the words Change PC Settings along the bottom to open the Start screen's mini-Control Panel.

Tap a Charms bar icon, and Windows gives a hint as to its purpose. For example, tapping the Settings area's Screen icon on a tablet presents a sliding bar for adjusting the screen's brightness. Sitting atop the sliding bar is a lock icon that keeps the screen from rotating, which is handy for reading e-books.

## *Introducing your free apps*

The Windows 8 Start screen comes stocked with several free apps, each living on its own square or rectangular tile. Every tile is labeled, so you know what's what. The tiles for some apps, known as *live tiles,* change constantly. The Finance app tile, for example, constantly updates with the stock market's latest swings; the Weather tile always tells you what to expect when you walk outdoors.

 The Windows 8 Start screen shows only some of your apps; to see them all, right-click a blank portion of the Start screen and choose All Apps from the screen's bottom.

You may spot some or all of the following apps on the list, ready to be launched at the click of a mouse or touch of a finger:

- ✔ **Calendar:** This lets you add your appointments or grab them automatically from calendars already created through accounts with Google or Hotmail.

- ✔ **Camera:** This lets you snap photos with your computer's built-in camera or webcam.

- ✔ **Desktop:** Choose this to fetch the traditional Windows desktop, which runs the Windows programs you've used for the past decade. I cover the desktop in Chapter 2.

- ✔ **Finance:** A live tile, this shows a 30-minute delay of the Dow, NASDAQ, and S&P. Choose Finance to see the usual charts and graphs of fear and uncertainty.

- ✔ **Games:** Designed mostly for Xbox 360 owners, this app lets you see your friends and gaming achievements. You can explore new games, watch game trailers, and buy new games for your console.

- ✔ **Internet Explorer:** This mini-version of Internet Explorer browses the web full screen, with nothing to get in the way: no menus, no tabs, just you and the current page. (When you're through, press the ⊞ key on your keyboard to return to the Start screen.)

- ✔ **Mail:** Covered in Chapter 5, this lets you send and receive e-mail. If you enter a Hotmail, Outlook, or Google account, the Mail app sets itself up automatically, stocking your People list, as well.

- ✔ **Maps:** Handy for trip planning, the Maps app brings up a version of Microsoft Bing Maps.

- ✔ **Messaging:** Covered in Chapter 5, this app lets you send text messages to friends through Facebook, Microsoft's Instant Messenger, and other systems.

- ✔ **Music:** This plays music stored on your PC. But Microsoft hopes you'll buy music from its store, as well.

- ✔ **News:** Visit here to read the news of the day, compiled from news services.

- ✔ **People:** The beauty of the People app, covered in Chapter 5, comes from its openness. Once you enter your accounts — Facebook, Twitter,

Google, and others — the People app grabs all your contacts, as well as their information, and stocks itself automatically.

✔ **Photos:** Covered in Chapter 6, the Photos app displays photos stored in your computer, as well as on accounts you may have on Facebook, Flickr, or SkyDrive.

✔ **Reader:** This handy app reads documents stored in the Adobe Portable Document Format (PDF). It jumps into action when you try to open any file stored in that document. (Most manuals available on websites come in PDF format; you can also find them attached to some e-mails.)

✔ **SkyDrive:** This term describes the Microsoft Internet cubbyhole where you can store your files. By storing them online in SkyDrive, covered in Chapter 3, you can access them from any Internet-connected computer.

✔ **Sports:** You can find sports news and scores here, as well as a way to add listings for your favorite sports teams.

✔ **Store:** Covered in Chapter 4, the Windows Store is the only way to add more apps on your Start screen. (Programs you install through your Windows desktop also add shortcuts to the Start screen.)

✔ **Travel:** Resembling a travel agent's billboard, this app lists travel hotspots, complete with maps, panoramic photos, reviews, and links for booking flights and hotels.

✔ **Video:** This works more like a video rental store, with a small button that lets you watch videos stored on your computer.

✔ **Weather:** This weather station forecasts a week's worth of weather in your area, but only if you grant it permission to access your location information. (Unless your computer has a GPS — Global Positioning System — the app narrows down your location by closest city rather than street address.)

The bundled Windows 8 apps work well within the confines of the Start screen. Unfortunately, Microsoft configured the Windows 8 desktop to use some of these Start screen apps rather than standard desktop programs.

# Exiting from Windows

Here's the quickest way to turn off your PC:

1. **Move your mouse pointer to the bottom-right corner to fetch the Charms bar. (On a touch-screen, swipe inward from the right edge.)**

2. **Click the Settings icon and then click the Power icon.**

3. **Choose Shut Down.**

   If the computer protests, saying you'll lose unsaved work, choose Sleep instead.

# Chapter 2

# The Traditional Desktop

● ● ● ● ● ● ● ● ● ● ● ● ● ● ● ● ● ● ● ● ● ● ● ● ● ● ● ● ● ● ● ●

## In This Chapter

▶ Finding the desktop

▶ Finding the Start screen

▶ Touching the desktop on a touchscreen

▶ Working on the desktop

▶ Retrieving deleted items from the Recycle Bin

▶ Working with the taskbar

● ● ● ● ● ● ● ● ● ● ● ● ● ● ● ● ● ● ● ● ● ● ● ● ● ● ● ● ● ● ● ●

*T*he app-filled world of Windows 8 works fine for couch-top computing. Without leaving your Start screen, you can listen to music, check your e-mail, watch the latest funny cat videos, and see whether anything particularly embarrassing has surfaced on Facebook.

But when Monday morning inevitably rolls around, it's time to switch gears.

## Finding the Desktop

The Windows 8 Start screen treats the desktop as just another *app:* a small, single-purpose program. So, you open the desktop just as you'd open any other app: Click the Start screen's Desktop tile.

The Desktop tile looks like a miniature version of your *real* desktop, complete with your current desktop background. When summoned, the desktop pushes aside the Start screen and fills the screen, ready to run your traditional Windows programs.

The Windows 8 desktop works much like the desktop found in previous Windows versions. Shown in Figure 2-1, the Windows 8 desktop is almost indistinguishable from the one in the previous version, Windows 7.

Point and click here to return to your last-used app.

Recycle Bin

Hover the mouse in either of these two corners to see the Charms bar and click its icons.

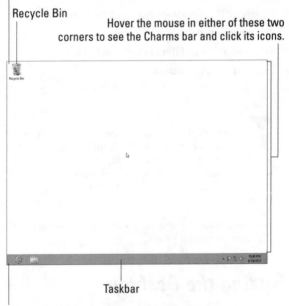

Taskbar

Point and click here to return to the Start screen.

**Figure 2-1:** The Windows 8 desktop lacks a Start button but otherwise looks identical to Windows 7.

The desktop, with its tiny buttons and thin bars, works best with a keyboard and mouse. If you're using Windows on a touchscreen tablet, you'll probably want to buy a portable mouse and keyboard for desktop work.

The Windows 8 desktop will run nearly all the Windows programs that ran on your old Windows XP, Windows Vista, or Windows 7 computer. Exceptions are antivirus programs, security suites, and some utility programs. Those don't usually transfer well from one Windows version to another.

## Touching the Desktop on a Touchscreen

Fingers work well for tapping the Start screen's extra-large tiles. And if you grimace enough, your touchscreen's touch controls will still work on the desktop's tiny buttons and thin borders. Here's how to control the desktop with your fingers:

- ✔ **Select:** To select something on the desktop, tap it with a fingertip; the pad of your finger may be too large.

- ✔ **Double-click:** To double-click something, tap it twice. Again, your fingertip works best.

- ✔ **Right-click:** To right-click an item, press your fingertip gently on it and wait for a small square to appear onscreen. When the square appears, remove your finger, and the pop-up menu stays on the screen. Then you can tap your desired option on the menu.

If your fingertip seems too wide for delicate desktop window maneuvers, you may yearn for an old-fashioned mouse and keyboard. Anticipating your frustration, all Windows 8 tablets include at least one USB port for plugging in either a mouse *or* a keyboard. To use both simultaneously, you have two options:

✔ **Buy a USB hub:** This inexpensive, small, USB-port stuffed box includes a short cable that plugs into your tablet's USB port. Plug your mouse and keyboard into two of the hub's ports, and you've transformed your tablet into a full-fledged desktop PC.

✔ **Buy a Bluetooth mouse and keyboard:** This age-old wireless technology comes in handy because *all* Windows 8 tablets still support Bluetooth. Bluetooth allows gadgets to connect wirelessly within about a 20-foot range. Buy a Bluetooth mouse and keyboard to use with your tablet, and you've saved your tablet's lone USB port for flash drives, printers, or other necessities.

With a pocket-sized mouse and portable keyboard, your tablet turns into two computers: the lightweight Start screen apps for casual computing and the full Windows desktop for doing some *real* work.

# Working with the Desktop

Start screen apps hog the entire screen, making it difficult to multitask. The desktop, by contrast, lets you run several programs simultaneously, each living within its own little *window.* That lets you spread several programs across the screen, easily sharing bits of information between them.

No matter how you use the desktop, it comes with four main parts, labeled earlier in Figure 2-1:

✔ **Start screen:** Although hidden, you can fetch the Start screen by pointing your mouse at the very bottom-left corner and clicking the Start screen thumbnail. (A press of the ■ key returns you to the Start screen, as well.) When summoned, the Start screen still lets you choose programs to run on your desktop.

✔ **Taskbar:** Resting lazily along the desktop's bottom edge, the taskbar lists the desktop programs and files you currently have open, as well as icons for a few favored programs. (Point at a program's icon on the taskbar to see the program's name or perhaps a thumbnail photo of that program in action.)

✔ **Recycle Bin:** The desktop's *Recycle Bin,* that wastebasket-shaped icon, stores your recently deleted files for easy retrieval. Whew!

✔ **Charms bar:** Technically, the shortcut-filled Charms bar isn't part of the desktop; it lives *everywhere* in Windows 8, hidden beyond every screen's right edge. To summon the Charms bar with a mouse, point at your desktop's top- or bottom-right corner.

Here are a few desktop tricks that may help you:

✔ You can start new projects directly from your desktop: Right-click a blank part of the desktop, choose New, and choose the project of your dreams from the pop-up menu, be it loading a favorite program or creating a folder to store new files. (The New menu lists most of your computer's programs, allowing you to avoid a laborious journey back to the Start screen.)

✔ Are you befuddled about some desktop object's reason for being? Timidly rest the pointer over the mysterious doodad, and Windows pops up a little box explaining what that thing is or does. Right-click the object, and the ever-helpful Windows 8 usually tosses up a menu listing nearly everything you can do with that particular object. This trick works on most icons and buttons found on your desktop and its programs.

✔ All the icons on your desktop may suddenly disappear, leaving it completely empty. Chances are good that Windows 8 hid them in a misguided attempt to be helpful. To bring your work back to life, right-click your empty desktop and choose View from the pop-up menu. Finally, make sure the Show Desktop Icons menu option has a check mark so everything stays visible.

## Summoning the Start screen and open apps

The Start button no longer lives in the desktop's bottom-left corner. Now, simply pointing and clicking at that little corner of desktop real estate fetches the new Windows 8 Start *screen*. When the Start screen appears, you click the app or program you'd like to run. To visit the Start screen from the desktop, as well as to revisit any recently opened apps, follow these steps:

1. **Point the mouse cursor at your screen's bottom-left corner.**

   A tiny thumbnail-sized Start screen icon rears its head, shown in the bottom-left corner of Figure 2-2. Click it to return to the Start screen.

   Or, if you want to return to any currently running apps, move to the next step.

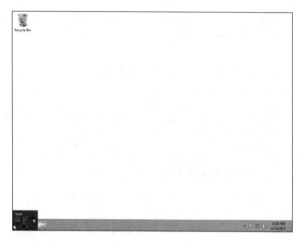

**Figure 2-2:** Point at the bottom-left corner to reveal an icon that takes you to the Start screen.

2. **When the Start screen icon appears, slowly raise your mouse pointer along the screen's left edge.**

   As you move the pointer up the screen's edge, thumbnails of your open apps appear, leaving you with several choices:

   • To return to an open app, click its thumbnail. The desktop disappears, and the app fills the screen, looking just as you last left it.

   • To return to the desktop from any app, head for the Start screen and click the Desktop tile. Or, if you spot a Desktop thumbnail among the list of recently used apps, click the Desktop thumbnail to return to the desktop.

   • To close an open app, right-click its thumbnail and choose Close. The app disappears from the screen, leaving you at the desktop.

You can also fetch the Start screen by pressing the ⊞ key on your keyboard or tablet.

## *Cleaning up a messy desktop*

When icons cover your desktop like a year's worth of sticky notes, Windows 8 offers several ways to clean up the mess. If you simply want your desktop clutter to look more organized — lined up straight or in organized piles, for example — then do this: Right-click the desktop and choose Sort By from the pop-up menu. The submenu offers these choices:

- ✔ **Name:** Arrange all icons in alphabetical order using neat, vertical rows.

- ✔ **Size:** Arrange icons according to their size, placing the smallest ones at the top of the rows.

- ✔ **Item Type:** This lines up icons by their *type*. All photographs are grouped together, for example, as are all links to websites.

- ✔ **Date Modified:** Arrange icons by the date you or your PC last changed them.

Right-clicking the desktop and choosing the View option lets you change the desktop icons' size, as well as play with these desk-organizing options:

- ✔ **Auto Arrange Icons:** Automatically arrange everything in vertical rows — even newly positioned icons are swept into tidy rows.

- ✔ **Align Icons to Grid:** Turned on by default, this option places an invisible grid on the screen and aligns all icons within the grid's borders to keep them nice and tidy — no matter how hard you try to mess them up.

✔ **Show Desktop Icons:** Always keep this option turned on. When turned off, Windows hides every icon on your desktop. If you can remember in your frustration, click this option again to toggle your icons back on.

✔ **Show Desktop Gadgets:** Gadgets are little things like clocks and weather forecasters you can add to your desktop. Introduced in Windows Vista and Windows 7 but rarely used, they've been replaced by apps.

Most View options are also available within any of your folders. To find them, click any folder's View tab that lives along its top edge.

## *Jazzing up the desktop's background*

To jazz up your desktop, Windows 8 covers it with a pretty picture known as a *background*. (Many people refer to the background simply as *wallpaper*.) When you tire of the built-in scenery, feel free to replace it with a picture stored on your computer:

1. **Right-click a blank part of the desktop, choose Personalize, and click the Desktop Background option in the window's bottom-left corner.**

2. **Click any one of the pictures, shown in Figure 2-3, and Windows 8 quickly places it onto your desktop's background.**

   Found a keeper? Click the Save Changes button to keep it on your desktop. Or, if you're still searching, move to the next step.

3. **Click the Browse button to see photos inside your Pictures library or My Pictures folder.**

   Most people store their digital photos in their Pictures library or My Pictures folder.

**Figure 2-3:** Try different backgrounds by clicking them; click the Browse button to see pictures from different folders.

4. **Click different pictures to see how they look as your desktop's background.**

When you find a background you like, you're done. Exit the program with a click in its upper-right corner, and your chosen photo drapes across your desktop.

Here are some tips on changing your desktop's background:

✔ Options listed in the Picture Position section let you choose whether the image should be *tiled* repeatedly across the screen, *centered* directly in the middle, or *stretched* to fill the entire screen. The Tile, Fill, and Fit options work best with small photos, such as those taken with cellphones, by repeating or enlarging them to fit the screen's borders.

✔ The desktop's Internet Explorer web browser can easily borrow any picture found on the Internet for a background. Right-click on the

website's picture and choose Set as Background
from the pop-up menu. Microsoft sneakily
copies the image onto your desktop as its new
background.

✔ If a background photograph makes your desktop icons too difficult to see, splash your desktop with a single color instead: After Step 1 of
the preceding list, click the Picture Location
box's down arrow. When the drop-down list
appears, select Solid Colors. Choose your favorite color to have it fill your desktop.

✔ To change the entire *look* of Windows 8, right-
click on the desktop, choose Personalize, and
select a theme. Aimed at heavy-duty procrasti-
nators, different themes splash different colors
across the various Windows buttons, borders,
and boxes.

## Snapping an app alongside the desktop

Windows 8 normally keeps the Start screen and the
desktop separated into two distinct worlds. You can
work within the Start screen or within the desktop,
but not both. Sometimes, though, that's not good
enough.

For example, you may want to see the Start screen's
Calendar app resting alongside your desktop to
remind you of your day's commitments. Or perhaps
you need your Messenger app open while you work,
so you can consult a friend on a name for your latest
jazz band. The solution is to *snap* your app alongside
the desktop: The app consumes less than one-quarter
of the screen, while the desktop fills the rest, as
shown in Figure 2-4. Or, you can give your app the
larger screen portion, shrinking the desktop.

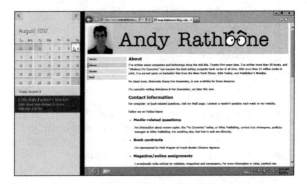

**Figure 2-4:** Snapping an app (placing it alongside your desktop) lets you view an app from the desktop.

To snap an app on your desktop, follow these steps:

1. **Open any Start screen app.**

   To reach the Start screen, press the ▦ key. Or, using a mouse, point at the bottom-left corner of your desktop and click when the Start screen icon appears. Then open an app you want to snap alongside the desktop.

   If you're using a mouse or touchscreen, jump ahead to Step 3.

2. **If you're using a keyboard, hold down the ▦ key and press the period key.**

   The app snaps to the left of your screen. Press ▦ + . (period) again to snap the app to the screen's *right* edge, instead. If you don't see the desktop along the app's side, move to Step 3; the desktop will open alongside the docked app.

3. **Switch back to the desktop.**

   To return to the desktop, hold down the ▦ key and press D, or click the Start screen's Desktop tile.

4. **Snap the app of your choosing against your desktop.**

   These steps are much simpler to *do* than read. But here goes:

   - **Mouse:** Point at the screen's top- or bottom-left corner until a thumbnail of your most recently used app appears. Right-click the desired app and, from the pop-up menu, choose Snap Left or Snap Right to snap the app to the screen side of your choosing.

   - **Touchscreen:** Slowly drag your finger from the left edge of the screen inward; your most recently opened app appears, following along with the motion of your finger. When a vertical strip appears onscreen, lift your finger, and the app snaps itself to the screen's left edge.

When the app snaps against the desktop's edge, it leaves a vertical bar separating it from your desktop. When the app snaps against the desktop's edge, it stays there, even if you switch to the Start screen or load other apps.

Although app snapping works well for a few tasks, it comes with more rules than a librarian:

✔ To *unsnap* the app, drag that vertical bar toward the screen's edge. Or press ⊞ + . (period) until the app disappears.

✔ When the app sticks to the side, you can drag the vertical bar inward, making the app fill most of the screen and turning the desktop into a rather useless little strip.

✔ To toggle the app from one edge to another, press ⊞ + . (period); the app switches sides. Press ⊞ + . (period) again, and the app unsnaps from the edge.

✔ You can't snap an app to the side of the Start screen. The Start screen *always* consumes the entire screen. But when you switch away from the Start screen, the previously snapped app will still be in place, clinging to its same edge.

✔ You can only snap *one* app at a time. For example, you can't snap an app onto each side of your desktop.

✔ You can snap apps only on a screen with a resolution of at least 1366 x 768. In human language, that means an *extra-wide* computer screen, which you won't find on most netbooks or older laptops. You *will* find that resolution, however, on all Windows 8 tablets.

✔ To see your screen's resolution, open the desktop by pressing ⊞ + D. Right-click a blank part of your desktop and choose Screen Resolution from the pop-up menu. You can select your resolution from the Resolution drop-down scroll bar. (You should usually choose the highest resolution offered.)

## *Dumpster diving in the Recycle Bin*

The Recycle Bin, that wastebasket icon in the corner of your desktop, works much like a *real* recycle bin. It lets you retrieve the discarded coupons you thought you'd never need. You can dump something from the desktop — a file or folder, for example — into the Windows 8 Recycle Bin in either of these ways:

✔ Simply right-click on the unwanted item and choose Delete from the menu. Windows 8 asks cautiously if you're *sure* that you want to delete the item. Click Yes, and Windows 8 dumps it into the Recycle Bin, just as if you'd dragged it there. Whoosh!

✔ For a quick deletion rush, click the unwanted object and poke your Delete key.

Want something back? Double-click the Recycle Bin icon to see your recently deleted items. Right-click the item you want and choose Restore.

To delete something *permanently,* just delete it from inside the Recycle Bin: Click it and press the Delete key. To delete *everything* in the Recycle Bin, right-click the Recycle Bin icon and choose Empty Recycle Bin.

 To bypass the Recycle Bin completely when deleting files, hold down Shift while pressing Delete. Poof! The deleted object disappears, ne'er to be seen again — a handy trick when dealing with sensitive items, such as credit-card numbers or late-night love letters meant for a nearby cubicle dweller.

✔ The Recycle Bin icon changes from an empty wastepaper basket to a full one as soon as it's holding any deleted file or files.

✔ Your Recycle Bin keeps your deleted files until the garbage consumes about 5 percent of your hard drive space. Then it purges your oldest deleted files to make room for the new. If you're low on hard drive space, shrink the bin's size by right-clicking the Recycle Bin and choosing Properties. Decrease the Custom Size number to purge the bin more quickly; increase the number, and the Recycle Bin hangs onto files a little longer.

 ✔ The Recycle Bin saves only items deleted from your *own* computer's drives. That means it won't save anything deleted from a CD, memory card, MP3 player, flash drive, or digital camera.

> ✔ If you delete something from somebody else's computer over a network, it can't be retrieved. The Recycle Bin holds only items deleted from your *own* computer, not somebody else's computer. (For some awful reason, the Recycle Bin on the other person's computer doesn't save the item, either.) Be careful.

## Bellying Up to the Taskbar

Whenever more than one window sits across your desktop, you face a logistics problem: Programs and windows tend to overlap, making them difficult to spot. To make matters worse, programs such as Internet Explorer and Microsoft Word can each contain several windows apiece. How do you keep track of all the windows?

The Windows 8 solution is the *taskbar* — a special area that keeps track of your currently running programs and their windows. Shown in Figure 2-5, the taskbar lives along the bottom of your desktop, constantly updating itself to show an icon for every currently running program.

**Figure 2-5:** Click buttons for currently running programs on the taskbar.

Not sure what a taskbar icon does? Rest your mouse pointer over any of the taskbar's icons to see either the program's name or a thumbnail image of the program's contents, as shown in Figure 2-5. In that figure, for example, you can see that Internet Explorer contains two web pages.

From the taskbar, you can perform powerful magic, as described in the following list:

- ✔ **To play with a program listed on the task-bar, click its icon.** Whenever you load a program on the desktop, its icon automatically appears on the taskbar. If one of your open windows ever gets lost on your desktop, click its icon on the taskbar to bring it to the forefront. Clicking the taskbar icon yet again minimizes that same window.

- ✔ **To close a window listed on the taskbar, *right-click* its icon and choose Close from the pop-up menu.** The program quits, just as if you'd chosen its Exit command from within its own window.

- ✔ **Traditionally, the taskbar lives along your desktop's bottom edge, but you can move it to any edge you want, a handy space saver on extra-wide monitors. (*Hint:* Try dragging it to your screen's side. If it doesn't move, right-click the taskbar and click Lock the Taskbar to remove the check mark by that option.)**

- ✔ **If the taskbar keeps hiding below the screen's bottom edge, point the mouse at the screen's bottom edge until the taskbar surfaces.** Then right-click the taskbar, choose Properties, and remove the check mark from Auto-Hide the Taskbar.

✔ **You can add your favorite programs directly to the taskbar.** From the Start screen, right-click the favored program's tile and choose Pin to Taskbar. The program's icon then lives on the taskbar for easy access, just as if it were running. Tired of the program hogging space on your taskbar? Right-click it and choose Unpin This Program from Taskbar.

## Clicking the taskbar's sensitive areas

Here's the lowdown on the icons near the taskbar's right edge, shown in Figure 2-6, known as the *notification area.* Different items appear in the notification area depending on your PC and programs, but you'll probably encounter some of these:

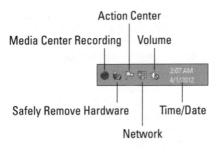

Action Center

Media Center Recording    Volume

Safely Remove Hardware    Time/Date

Network

**Figure 2-6:** The taskbar's tiny icons along the right edge mostly show items running in the background on your PC.

**Minimize Windows:** This small strip (see pointer in the margin), hidden against the taskbar's far-right edge, instantly minimizes all open windows when you click it. (Click it again to put the windows back in place.)

**Time/Date:** Click the time and date to fetch a handy monthly calendar and clock. If you want to change the time or date, or even add a second time zone, click the Time/Date area and choose Change Date and Time Settings.

**Windows Media Center Recording:** The glowing red circle means Windows Media Center, available separately as an add-on, is currently recording something off the television.

**Media Center Guide Listings:** Media Center is downloading the latest TV listings.

**Safely Remove Hardware:** Before unplugging a storage device, be it a tiny flash drive, a portable music player, or a portable hard drive, click here. That tells Windows to prepare the gadget for unplugging.

**Action Center:** Indicates that Windows wants you to do something, be it to click a permission window, install an antivirus program, check your last backup, or perform some other important task.

**Wired Network:** This appears when you're connected to the Internet or other PCs through a wired network. Not connected? A red X appears over the icon.

**Wireless Network:** Your PC is wirelessly connected to the Internet or other network. When all five bars show, you have a very strong signal.

**Volume:** Click or tap this ever-so-handy little speaker icon to adjust your PC's volume.

**Windows Problem Reporting:** When Windows runs into trouble, this icon appears; click it to see possible solutions.

**Windows Automatic Updates:** This icon appears when Windows downloads *updates,* usually small programs designed to fix your PC, from Microsoft's website at Windows Update.

**Task Manager:** Coveted by computer technicians, this little program can end misbehaving programs, monitor background tasks, monitor performance, and do other stuff of techie dreams.

**Windows Host Process:** This dismally named icon delivers an even worse message: Your newly plugged-in gadget won't work, be it your printer, scanner, music player, or other item. Try unplugging the device, running its installation software again, and plugging it back in.

**Explorer:** Older PCs come with two types of USB ports: fast and slow. This icon means you've plugged a speedy gadget into your slow port. Try unplugging it and plugging it into a different port. (The USB ports on a desktop computer's back side are often the faster ones.)

**Power, Outlet:** This shows that your laptop is plugged into an electrical outlet and is charging its battery.

**Power, Battery:** Your laptop or tablet is running on batteries only. (Rest your mouse pointer over the icon to see how much power remains.)

**Arrow:** Sometimes the taskbar hides things. If you see a tiny upward-pointing arrow at the start of the taskbar's notification area, click it to see a few hidden icons slide out.

Get familiar with these icons, and you'll find that using the notification area is a snap!

# Chapter 3

# Storage: Internal, External, and in the Sky

· · · · · · · · · · · · · · · · · · · · · · · · · · · · · · · · · · · · ·

## In This Chapter

▶ Managing files with the desktop's File Explorer

▶ Navigating drives, folders, and flash drives

▶ Understanding libraries

▶ Creating and naming folders

▶ Selecting and deselecting items

▶ Copying and moving files and folders

▶ Writing to CDs and memory cards

▶ Understanding Windows SkyDrive

· · · · · · · · · · · · · · · · · · · · · · · · · · · · · · · · · · · · ·

*F*olks hoped the new Start screen would simplify their work, finally transcending the complicated world of files and folders. Unfortunately, that's not the case. Insert a flash drive or plug your digital camera into your Windows 8 computer, and the Start screen dumps you onto the Windows desktop. There, File Explorer — Windows' age-old digital filing cabinet — rears its head.

This chapter explains how to use File Explorer to navigate the files, folders, and drives on your PC. It also helps you work with CDs, memory cards, and the new Windows SkyDrive storage area.

# Browsing the File Explorer

To keep your programs and files neatly arranged, Windows cleaned up the squeaky old file cabinet metaphor with whisper-quiet Windows icons. Inside File Explorer, the icons represent your computer's storage areas, allowing you to copy, move, rename, or delete your files before the investigators arrive.

To see your computer's file cabinets — called *drives* or *disks* in computer lingo — open the Start screen's File Explorer tile. The Start screen vanishes, and the Windows desktop appears, with your files and folders listed in File Explorer. File Explorer can display its contents in many ways. To see your computer's storage areas, click the word Computer from the pane along the left edge.

The File Explorer image shown in Figure 3-1 will look slightly different from the one on your PC, but you'll still see the same basic sections, each described in the upcoming list.

The File Explorer window comes with these main parts:

**Navigation Pane:** The handy Navigation Pane, that strip along the left edge, lists shortcuts to special folders called *libraries* that hold your most valuable computerized possessions: your Documents, Music, Pictures, and Videos.

 **Hard Disk Drives:** Shown in Figure 3-1, this area lists your PC's *hard drives* — your biggest storage areas. Every computer has at least one hard drive. Double-clicking a hard drive icon displays its files and folders, but you'll rarely find much useful information when probing that way. No, your most important files live in your Documents, Music, Pictures, and Videos libraries, which live one click away on the Navigation Pane.

Notice the hard drive bearing the little Windows icon (shown in the margin)? That means Windows 8 lives on that drive. The more colored space you see in the line next to each hard drive's icon, the more files you've stuffed onto your drive. When the line turns red, your drive is almost full, and you should think about upgrading to a larger drive.

**Devices with Removable Storage:** This area shows detachable storage gadgetry attached to your computer. Some of the more common ones include CD, DVD, and Blu-ray drives; memory card readers and flash drives; MP3 players; and digital cameras.

Windows
Media Player
**Network Location:** This icon in the margin, seen only by people who've linked groups of PCs into a *network*, represents the Media Player library living on another PC. Click one of these icons to access the music, photos, and video stored on those other PCs.

**Figure 3-1:** The File Explorer window displays your computer's storage areas.

If you plug a digital camcorder, cellphone, or other gadget into your PC, the File Explorer window will often sprout a new icon representing your gadget. If Windows neglects to ask what you'd like to do with your newly plugged-in gadget, right-click the icon; you see a list of everything you can do with that item. No icon? Then you need to install a *driver* for your gadget.

# Getting the Lowdown on Folders and Libraries

A *folder* is a storage area on a drive, just like a real folder in a file cabinet. Windows 8 divides your computer's hard drives into many folders to separate your many projects. For example, you store all your music in your My Music folder and your pictures in your My Pictures folder.

A *library,* by contrast, is a super folder. Instead of showing the contents of a single folder, it shows the contents of *several* folders. For example, your Music library shows the tunes living in your *My* Music folder, as well as the tunes in your *Public* Music folder. (The Public Music folder contains music available to everyone who uses your PC.)

Windows 8 gives you four libraries for storing your files and folders. For easy access, they live in the Navigation Pane along the left side of every folder. Figure 3-2 shows your libraries: Documents, Music, Pictures, and Videos.

**Figure 3-2:** Windows 8 provides every person with these same four libraries, but it keeps everybody's folders separate.

# Peering into Your Drives, Folders, and Libraries

Put on your hard hat to go spelunking among your computer's drives, folders, and libraries. You can use this section as your guide.

## Seeing the files on a disk drive

Like everything else in Windows 8, disk drives are represented by buttons, or icons. The File Explorer program also shows information stored in other areas, such as the contents of connected MP3 players, digital cameras, or scanners. Opening an icon usually lets you access the device's contents and move files back and forth, just as you would do with any other folder in Windows 8.

When you double-click a hard drive icon in File Explorer, Windows 8 promptly opens the drive to show you the folders packed inside. But how should Windows react when you insert something new into your computer, such as a CD, DVD, or flash drive?

Earlier versions of Windows tried to second-guess you. When you inserted a music CD, for example, Windows automatically began playing the music. The more polite Windows 8, by contrast, asks how you want it to handle the situation, as shown in Figure 3-3. The same message appears whether you're working within the desktop or Start screen.

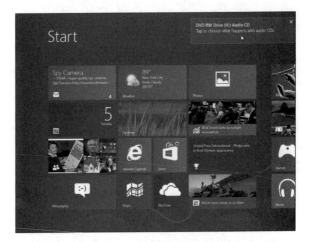

**Figure 3-3:** Windows 8 asks how it should handle newly inserted items.

When you see a message like the one shown in the upper-right corner of Figure 3-3, select the message with a click of the mouse. A second message appears, shown in Figure 3-4, that lists everything you can do with that item. Choose one of the options, and Windows 8 behaves this way the next time you insert a similar item.

**Figure 3-4:** Choose how Windows 8 should react the next time you insert a particular item, such as a CD.

## Seeing what's inside a folder

Because folders are really little storage compartments, Windows 8 uses a picture of a little folder to represent a place for storing files. To see what's inside a folder, either in File Explorer or on the Windows 8 desktop, just double-click that folder's picture. A new window pops up, showing that folder's contents. Spot another folder inside that folder? Double-click that one to see what's inside. Keep clicking until you find what you want or reach a dead end.

Reached a dead end? If you mistakenly end up in the wrong folder, back your way out as if you're browsing the web. Click the Back arrow at the window's top-left corner. (It's the same arrow that appears in the margin.) That closes the wrong folder and shows you the folder you just left. If you keep clicking the Back arrow, you end up right where you started.

The Address Bar provides another quick way to jump to different places in your PC. As you move from folder to folder, the folder's Address Bar — that little word-filled box at the folder's top — constantly keeps track of your trek.

Notice the little arrows between the folder names.
Those little arrows provide quick shortcuts to other
folders and windows. Try clicking any of the arrows;
menus appear, listing the places you can jump to
from that point. For example, click the arrow after
Libraries, shown in Figure 3-5, and a menu drops
down, letting you jump quickly to your other
libraries.

**Figure 3-5:** Click the arrow after Libraries to jump to another
place in the folder.

# Creating a New Folder

To store new information in Windows 8 — a new
batch of letters to the hospital's billing department,
for example — you create a new folder, think up a
name for the new folder, and start stuffing it with files.

To create a new folder quickly, click Home from the
folder's toolbar buttons and choose New Folder from
the Ribbon menu. If you can't find the right menus,
though, here's a quick and foolproof method:

1. **Right-click inside your folder (or on the desktop) and choose New.**

2. **From the resulting side menu, select Folder.**

   When you choose Folder, shown in Figure 3-6, a
   new folder quickly appears, waiting for you to
   type a new name.

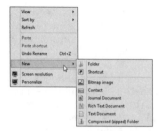

**Figure 3-6:** Creating a new folder where you want it.

3. **Type a new name for the folder.**

   A newly created folder bears the boring name of New Folder. When you begin typing, Windows 8 quickly erases the old name and fills in your new name. Done? Save the new name by either pressing Enter or clicking somewhere away from the name you've just typed.

   If you mess up the name and want to try again, right-click the folder, choose Rename, and start over.

   Certain symbols are banned from folder (and file) names. The "Using legal folder names and filenames" sidebar spells out the details, but you never have trouble when using plain old letters and numbers for names.

# Renaming a File or Folder

Sick of a file or folder's name? Then change it. Just right-click the offending icon and choose Rename from the menu that pops up. Windows highlights the file's old name, which disappears as you begin typing the new one. Press Enter or click the desktop when you're through, and you're off. Or you can click the filename or folder name to select it, wait a second, and click the name again to change it. Some people click the name and press F2; Windows automatically lets you rename the file or folder.

When you rename a file, only its name changes. The contents are still the same, the file is still the same size, and the file is still in the same place. Renaming certain folders confuses Windows, especially if those folders contain programs. And please don't rename these folders: My Documents, My Pictures, My Music, or My Videos.

 To rename large groups of files simultaneously, select them all, right-click the first one, and choose Rename. Type in the new name and press Enter; Windows 8 renames that file. However, it also renames all your *other* selected files to the new name, adding a number as it goes: cat, cat (2), cat (3), cat (4), and so on. It's a handy way to rename photographs.

## Selecting Bunches of Files or Folders

Although selecting a file, folder, or other object may seem particularly boring, it swings the doors wide open for further tasks: deleting, renaming, moving, and copying, for example. To select a single item, just click it. To select several files and folders, hold down the Ctrl key when you click the names or icons. Each name or icon stays highlighted when you click the next one.

To gather several files or folders sitting next to each other in a list, click the first one. Then hold down the Shift key as you click the last one. Those two items are highlighted, along with every file and folder sitting between them.

Windows 8 lets you *lasso* files and folders as well. Point slightly above the first file or folder you want; then, while holding down the mouse button, point at the last file or folder. The mouse creates a colored lasso to surround your files. Let go of the mouse button, and the lasso disappears, leaving all the surrounded files highlighted.

To quickly select all the files in a folder, choose Select All from the folder's Edit menu. (No menu? Then select them by pressing Ctrl+A.) Here's another nifty trick: To grab all but a few files, press Ctrl+A and, while still holding down Ctrl, click the ones you don't want.

## Getting Rid of a File or Folder

To delete a file, folder, shortcut, or just about anything else in Windows, right-click its name or icon. Then choose Delete from the pop-up menu. To delete in a hurry, click the offending object and press the Delete key. Dragging and dropping a file or folder to the Recycle Bin does the same thing.

The Delete option deletes entire folders, including any files or folders stuffed *inside* those folders. Make sure that you select the correct folder before you choose Delete.

After you choose Delete, Windows tosses a box in your face, asking whether you're *sure.* If you're sure, click Yes. If you're tired of Windows' cautious questioning, right-click the Recycle Bin, choose Properties, and remove the check mark next to Display Delete Confirmation Dialog. Windows now deletes any highlighted items whenever you — or an inadvertent brush of your shirt sleeve — press the Delete key.

 Be extra sure that you know what you're doing when deleting any file that has pictures of little gears in its icon. These files are usually sensitive hidden files, and the computer wants you to leave them alone.

 Icons with little arrows in their corner (like the one in the margin) are *shortcuts* — push buttons that merely load files. Deleting shortcuts deletes only a *button* that loads a file or program. The file or program itself remains undamaged and still lives inside your computer.

## *Copying or Moving Files and Folders*

To copy or move files to different folders on your hard drive, it's sometimes easiest to use your mouse to *drag* them there. For example, here's how to move a file to a different folder on your desktop. In this case, I'm moving the Traveler file from the House folder to the Morocco folder.

1. **Align the two windows next to each other.**

2. **Aim the mouse pointer at the file or folder you want to move.**

   In this case, point at the Traveler file.

3. **While holding down the right mouse button, move the mouse until it points at the destination folder.**

Moving the mouse drags the file along with it, and Windows 8 explains that you're moving the file. As shown in Figure 3-7, the Traveler file is being dragged from the House folder to the Morocco folder.

**Figure 3-7:** To move an item, drag it while holding down the right mouse button.

Always drag icons while holding down the *right* mouse button. Windows 8 is then gracious enough to give you a menu of options when you position the icon, and you can choose to copy, move, or create a shortcut. If you hold down the *left* mouse button, Windows 8 sometimes doesn't know whether you want to copy or move.

4. **Release the mouse button and choose Copy Here, Move Here, or Create Shortcuts Here from the pop-up menu.**

When dragging and dropping takes too much work, Windows offers a few other ways to copy or move files.

Depending on your screen's current layout, some of the following onscreen tools may work more easily:

- ✔ **Right-click menus:** Right-click a file or folder and choose Cut or Copy, depending on whether you want to move or copy it. Then right-click your destination folder and choose Paste. It's simple, it always works, and you needn't bother placing any windows side by side.

- ✔ **Ribbon commands:** In File Explorer, click your file or folder; then click the Ribbon's Home tab and choose Copy To (or Move To). A menu drops down, listing some common locations. Don't spot the right spot? Then click Choose Location, click through the drive and folders to reach the destination folder, and Windows transports the file accordingly. Although a bit cumbersome, this method works if you know the exact location of the destination folder.

- ✔ **Navigation Pane:** This panel along File Explorer's left edge lists popular locations: libraries, drives, and oft-used folders. That lets you drag and drop a file into a spot on the Navigation Pane, sparing you the hassle of opening a destination folder.

After you install a program on your computer, don't ever move that program's folder. Programs wedge themselves into Windows. Moving the program may break it, and you'll have to reinstall it. Feel free to move a program's *shortcut* (shortcut icons contain a little arrow), though.

# Writing to CDs and DVDs

Most computers today write information to CDs and DVDs using a flameless approach known as *burning*. To see whether you're stuck with an older drive that can't burn discs, remove any discs from inside the drive; then open File Explorer from the Start screen and look at the icon for your CD or DVD drive.

Because computers always speak in secret code, here's what you can do with the disc drives in your computer:

- ✔ **DVD-RW:** Read and write to CDs *and* DVDs.

- ✔ **BD-ROM:** Read and write to CDs and DVDs, plus read Blu-ray discs.

- ✔ **BD-RE:** These can read and write to CDs, DVDs, *and* Blu-ray discs.

 If your PC has two CD or DVD burners, tell Windows 8 which drive you want to handle your disc-burning chores: Right-click the drive, choose Properties, and click the Recording tab. Then choose your favorite drive in the top box.

## Buying the right kind of blank CDs and DVDs for burning

Stores sell two types of CDs: CD-R (short for CD-Recordable) and CD-RW (short for CD-ReWritable). Here's the difference:

- ✔ **CD-R:** Most people buy CD-R discs because they're very cheap and they work fine for storing music or files. You can write to them until they fill up; then you can't write to them anymore.

- ✔ **CD-RW:** Techies sometimes buy CD-RW discs for making temporary backups of data. You can write information to them, just like CD-Rs. But when a CD-RW disc fills up, you can erase it and start over with a clean slate.

DVDs come in both R and RW formats, just like CDs, so the preceding R and RW rules apply to them, as well. Most DVD burners sold in the past few years can write to any type of blank CD or DVD.

Buying blank DVDs for older drives is chaos: The manufacturers fought over which storage format to use, confusing things for everybody. To buy the right blank DVD, check your computer's receipt to see what formats its DVD burner needs: DVD-R, DVD-RW, DVD+R, or DVD+RW.

## Copying files to or from a CD or DVD

CDs and DVDs once hailed from the school of simplicity: You simply slid them into your CD player or DVD player. But as soon as those discs graduated to PCs, the problems grew. When you create a CD or DVD, you must tell your PC *what* you're copying and *where* you intend to play it: Music for a CD player? Photo slide shows for a TV's DVD player? Or files to store on your computer?

If you choose the wrong answer, your disc won't work, and you've created yet another coaster.

Here are the Disc Creation rules:

- ✔ **Music:** To create a CD that plays music in your CD player or car stereo, you need to fire up the Windows 8 Media Player program and burn an *audio CD.*

- ✔ **Photo slide shows:** Windows 8 no longer includes the Windows DVD Maker bundled with Windows Vista and Windows 7. To create photo slide-shows, you now need a third-party program.

If you just want to copy *files* to a CD or DVD, perhaps to save as a backup or to give to a friend, stick around.

Follow these steps to write files to a new, blank CD or DVD. (If you're writing files to a CD or DVD that you've written to before, jump ahead to Step 4.)

1. **Insert the blank disc into your disc burner. Then click or tap the Notification box that appears in the screen's upper-right corner.**

2. **When the Notification box asks how you'd like to proceed, click the box's Burn Files to Disc option.**

3. **In the resulting Burn a Disc dialog box, type a name for the disc, describe how you want to use the disc, and click Next.**

   Windows can burn the files to the disc two different ways:

   • **Like a USB flash drive:** This method lets you read and write files to the disc many times, a handy way to use discs as portable file carriers.

   • **With a CD/DVD player:** If you plan to play your disc on a fairly new home stereo disc player that's smart enough to read files stored in several different formats, select this method.

   Armed with the disc's name, Windows 8 prepares the disc for incoming files.

4. **Tell Windows 8 which files to write to disc.**

   Now that your disc is ready to accept the files, tell Windows 8 what information to send its way. You can do this in any of several ways:

   • Right-click the item you want to copy, be it a single file, folder, or selected files and folders.

When the pop-up menu appears, choose Send To and select your disc burner from the menu.

- Drag and drop files and/or folders on top of the burner's icon in File Explorer.

- From your My Music, My Pictures, or My Documents folder, click the Share tab and then click Burn to Disc. This button copies all of that folder's files (or just the files you've selected) to the disc as files.

- Tell your current program to save the information to the disc rather than to your hard drive.

No matter which method you choose, a progress window appears, showing the disc burner's progress. When the progress window disappears, Windows has finished burning the disc.

5. **Close your disc-burning session by ejecting the disc.**

When you're through copying files to the disc, push your drive's Eject button (or right-click the drive's icon in File Explorer and choose Eject).

 If you try to copy a large batch of files to a disc — more than will fit — Windows 8 complains immediately. Copy fewer files at a time, perhaps spacing them out over two discs.

 Most programs let you save files directly to disc. Choose Save from the File menu and select your CD burner. Put a disc (preferably one that's not already filled) into your disc drive to start the process.

# Working with Flash Drives and Memory Cards

Digital camera owners eventually become acquainted with *memory cards* — those little plastic squares that replaced the awkward rolls of film. Windows 8 can read digital photos directly from the camera after you find its cable and plug it into your PC. But Windows 8 can also grab photos straight off the memory card, a method praised by any owner who has lost her camera's cables.

The secret is a *memory card reader:* a little slot-filled box that stays plugged into your PC. Slide your memory card into the slot, and your PC can read the card's files, just like reading files from any other folder. Most office supply and electronics stores sell memory card readers that accept most popular memory card formats, and some computers even come with built-in card readers.

The beauty of card readers is that there's nothing new to figure out: Windows 8 treats your inserted card just like an ordinary folder. Insert your card, and a folder appears on your screen to show your digital camera photos. The same drag-and-drop and cut-and-paste rules covered earlier in this chapter still apply, letting you move the pictures or other files off the card and into a folder in your Pictures library.

Flash drives — also known as thumbdrives — work just like memory card readers. Plug the flash drive into one of your PC's USB ports, and the drive appears as an icon (shown in the margin) in File Explorer, ready to be opened with a double-click.

✔ First, the warning: Formatting a card or disk wipes out all its information. Never format a card or disk unless you don't care about the information it currently holds.

✔ Now, the procedure: If Windows complains that a newly inserted card isn't formatted, right-click its drive and choose Format. (This problem happens most often with brand-new or damaged cards.) Sometimes formatting also helps one gadget use a card designed for a different gadget — your digital camera may be able to use your MP3 player's card, for example.

# SkyDrive: Your Cubbyhole in the Clouds

Storing files inside your computer works fine while you're at home or work. And when leaving your computer, you can tote files on flash drives, CDs, DVDs, and portable hard drives — if you remember to grab them on the way out. But how can you access your files from *anywhere,* even if you've forgotten to pack them?

Microsoft's solution to that problem is called *SkyDrive.* Basically, it's your own private storage space on the Internet where you can dump your files and then retrieve them whenever you find an Internet connection. Romantic engineers refer to Internet-stashed files as *cloud storage.*

The Windows 8 Start screen comes with the free SkyDrive app, but you need a few extra things in order to use it:

✔ **Microsoft account:** You need a Microsoft account in order to upload or retrieve files to SkyDrive. Chances are, you created a Microsoft account when you first created your account on your Windows 8 PC. (I describe Microsoft accounts in Chapter 1.)

✔ **An Internet connection:** Without an Internet signal, either wireless or wired, your files stay floating in the clouds, away from you and your computer.

✔ **Patience:** Uploading files always takes longer than downloading files. Although you can upload small files fairly quickly, larger files like digital photos can take several minutes to upload.

## Accessing files with SkyDrive

To add, view, or download files you've stored on SkyDrive from the Start screen's SkyDrive app, as well as to add your own, follow these steps:

1. **From the Start screen, open the SkyDrive app.**

   When opened, the SkyDrive app (shown in Figure 3-8) may react any of several different ways depending on whether you've used SkyDrive before, and how.

   SkyDrive lists your stored folders along the left edge and your files along the right.

2. **To copy files from your computer to SkyDrive, choose Upload and locate the desired files on your computer.**

   To add files, right-click a blank part of the SkyDrive program; when the app's menu appears along the screen's bottom edge, choose Upload (shown in the margin). The Start screen's File Picker appears, shown in Figure 3-9, ready for you to choose the files you'd like to store in the clouds.

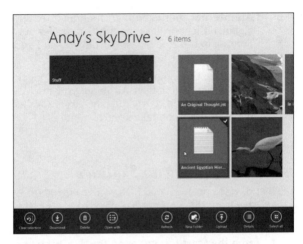

**Figure 3-8:** The SkyDrive app lets you keep files in a private Internet cubbyhole.

When you spot the folder containing the files you want, click it to open it and see its files.

3. **Choose the files you'd like to upload to SkyDrive.**

   Click the files you'd like to upload; if you click one by mistake, click it again to remove it from the upload list. Each time you click a file, SkyDrive adds the file to its upload list, shown along the app's bottom edge in Figure 3-9.

   Jump to another folder and click more files; SkyDrive adds those file to the list along the bottom, as well.

4. **Click the Add to SkyDrive button.**

   SkyDrive begins uploading your selected files to the sky. Documents float up there pretty quickly, but digital music and photos can take a lot of time.

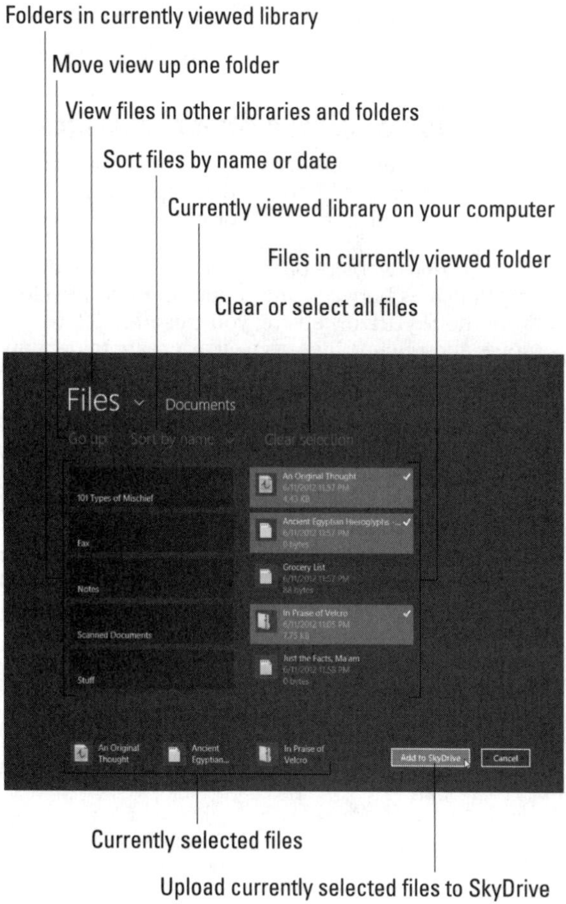

Folders in currently viewed library

Move view up one folder

View files in other libraries and folders

Sort files by name or date

Currently viewed library on your computer

Files in currently viewed folder

Clear or select all files

Currently selected files

Upload currently selected files to SkyDrive

**Figure 3-9:** Click the files to be sent to SkyDrive.

The SkyDrive app makes it fairly easy to open files you've already uploaded to the cloud, but it offers little control. For more features, visit SkyDrive from your desktop's web browser, a chore described in the next section.

## *Accessing SkyDrive from the desktop*

If the Start screen's SkyDrive app is too simple for your needs, head for the Windows desktop and visit the SkyDrive website at `http://skydrive.live.com`.

The SkyDrive website offers much more control when shuttling files between your computer and the cloud. From the SkyDrive website, you can add, delete, move, and rename files, as well as create folders and move files between folders.

For best results, use the SkyDrive website to upload and manage your files. After you've stocked SkyDrive with your favorite files, use the Start screen's SkyDrive app to access the particular files you need.

 For even more control over SkyDrive and your files, download the SkyDrive for Windows program from `http://apps.live.com/sky drive`. The desktop program creates a special folder on your computer that mirrors what's stored on SkyDrive. That makes SkyDrive particularly easy to use: Whenever you change the contents of that special folder on your computer, Windows automatically updates SkyDrive, as well.

# Chapter 4

# Working with Apps

. . . . . . . . . . . . . . . . . . . . . . . . . . . . .

## In This Chapter

▶ Opening a program, app, or document

▶ Installing and uninstalling apps

▶ Updating apps

▶ Seeing the apps you're currently running

. . . . . . . . . . . . . . . . . . . . . . . . . . . . .

*I*n Windows, *programs* and *apps* are your tools: Load a program or app, and you can add numbers, arrange words, and shoot spaceships. *Documents,* by contrast, are the things you create with apps and programs: tax forms, heartfelt apologies, and lists of high scores.

This chapter explains the basics of opening programs and apps from the new, tile-filled Start screen in Windows 8. It explains how to find and download a new app from the Start screen's Store app. It also tells you how to update or uninstall an app, and how to find any missing app or file.

## Starting a Program or App

Windows 8 banished the Start button from its oft-clicked spot on the desktop's bottom-left corner. Microsoft prefers to say, however, that it has *expanded* the Start button, turning it into a full-screen launching pad for your programs.

I explain the giant new Start screen, shown in Figure 4-1, in Chapter 1, as well as how to customize it, adding or removing tiles to ensure you find things more easily.

**Figure 4-1:** Click this Start screen and then click the tile for the program you want to open.

But even though the Start screen lives in a new place, it still lets you launch programs or apps by following these steps:

1. **Open the Start screen.**

   Because there's no longer a Start button, you can summon the Start screen any of these ways:

   • **Mouse:** Point your mouse in the screen's bottom-left corner and then click when the Start icon appears.

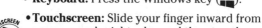 

- **Keyboard:** Press the Windows key (⊞).

 • **Touchscreen:** Slide your finger inward from your screen's right edge and then tap the Start icon.

The Start screen appears, refer to Figure 4-1, bringing a screen full of tiles representing many of your apps and programs.

2. **If you spot the tile for your program or app, choose it with a mouse click or, on a touchscreen, a tap of a finger.**

Don't see a tile for your sought-after program on the Start screen's list? Move to the next step.

3. **Scroll to the screen's right to see more tiles.**

The Start screen always opens to display the tiles on its farthest left edge. To see the apps and programs hiding from view, point at the screen's right edge with your mouse cursor; the rest of the Start screen's tiles begin scrolling into view.

 If you're a touchscreen owner, you can view the tiles by sliding your finger across the screen to the left.

4. **View *all* your apps.**

The Start screen shows apps first, followed by desktop programs. But to keep the list from stretching down the hallway, the Start screen doesn't list everything.

To reveal them *all*, right-click a blank part of the Start screen and then choose All Apps. All your apps appear listed by name and icon, followed by alphabetical lists of desktop programs, organized by categories. (Your most recently installed desktop programs always appear on the farthest right edge.)

 To see all your apps on a touchscreen, slide your finger upward from the screen's bottom edge and click the All Apps icon.

If you *still* can't find your program on the admittedly crowded Start screen, follow these tips for other ways to open an app or program:

- While you view the Start screen, begin typing the missing program's name. As you type the first letter, the Start screen clears, presenting a list of names beginning with that letter. Type a second or third letter, and the list of matches shrinks accordingly. When you spot the app or program you want, open it with a double-click (or a touch on a touchscreen.)

- Open File Explorer from the Start screen, choose Documents from the Navigation Pane along the window's left edge, and double-click the file you want to open. The correct program automatically opens with that file in tow.

- Double-click a *shortcut* to the program. Shortcuts, which often sit on your desktop, are handy, disposable buttons for launching files and folders.

- While you're on the desktop, you may spot the program's icon on the *taskbar* — a handy strip of icons lazily lounging along your desktop's bottom edge. If so, click the taskbar icon, and the program leaps into action.

- Right-click on the Windows desktop, choose New, and select the type of document you want to create. Windows 8 loads the right program for the job.

Windows offers other ways to open a program, but the preceding methods usually get the job done.

# *Adding and Deleting Apps*

 *Apps,* which are mini-programs specialized for single tasks, come from the world of *smartphones*: computerized cellphones. In fact, the apps in Windows 8 haven't cut their ties to the cellphone world. Apps you download for Windows 8 can also run on a Windows 8 cellphone.

Apps differ from traditional desktop programs in several ways:

- ✔ **Apps consume the entire screen;** programs run within windows on the desktop.

- ✔ **Apps are tied to your Microsoft account.** That means you need a Microsoft account to download a free or paid app from the Store app.

- ✔ **When you download an app from the Windows 8 Store app, you can run it on up to five PCs or devices** — as long as you're signed in to those PCs or devices with your Windows account.

- ✔ **Apps consume just one tile on the Start screen, thereby reducing Start screen bloat.** When installed, programs tend to sprinkle several tiles onto your Start screen.

Apps and programs can be created and sold by large companies, as well as by basement-dwelling hobbyists working in their spare time.

Although desktop programs and Start screen apps look and behave differently, Microsoft unfortunately refers to both as *apps* in Windows 8. You'll run across this terminology quirk when dealing with older programs, as well as newer programs created by companies not hip to Microsoft's new lingo.

## Adding new apps from the Store app

When you're tired of the apps bundled with Windows 8 or you need a new app to fill a special need, follow these steps to bring one into your computer.

1. **Open the Store app from the Start screen.**

   Don't see the Start screen? Press your keyboard's ⊞ key to whisk your way there.

   The Store app fills the screen, as shown in Figure 4-2.

**Figure 4-2:** The Store app lets you download apps to run from your Start screen.

   The Store opens to show the Spotlight category, but scrolling to the right reveals many more categories, such as Games, Books and Reference, News and Weather, and others.

2. **To narrow your search, choose a category by clicking its name.**

As you see more of the Store, you see several more ways to sort the available apps, as shown in Figure 4-3.

**Figure 4-3:** Narrow your search by subcategory, price, and rating.

3. **Sort by subcategory, price, and noteworthiness, and choose apps that look interesting.**

   For example, you can sort by subcategory, limiting the Games category to show only Card games.

   Some categories also let you sort by price, and you can choose Free, Paid, or Trial. And if you sort by noteworthiness, Microsoft shows you which apps are Newest, have the Highest Rating, or have the Lowest Price. (Hedge fund managers may sort by Highest Price, as well.)

4. **Choose any app to read a more detailed description.**

   A page opens to show more detailed information, including its price tag, pictures of the app, reviews left by previous customers, and more technical information.

5. **Click the Install, Buy, or Try button.**

   When you find a free app that you can't live with-out, click the Install button. Paid apps let you click either Buy or Try (a limited trial run). If you choose to install, try, or buy an app, its tile appears on your Start screen as quickly as your Internet connection speed allows.

Newly downloaded apps appear in a group on the Start screen's far-right edge.

## *Uninstalling apps*

Downloaded a dud app? To uninstall any app from the Start screen, right-click its tile. When the menu bar rises up from the screen's bottom edge, click Uninstall.

Uninstalling an app only removes that app from *your* account's Start screen. Your action won't affect other account holders who may have installed the app.

# *Updating Your Apps*

Programmers constantly tweak their apps, smoothing over rough spots, adding new features, and plugging security holes. When the program releases an update for your app, the Store tells you about it by putting a number on the Store app's tile.

To grab any waiting updates, visit the Start screen's Store app. Then click the word Update(s) in the top-right corner. The Store lists all the apps requiring updates; click Update All to bring them all up-to-date.

*Note:* When you update an app, it's not updated for
every account holder on the computer. Each person
has to update it for him- or herself. That holds true
for apps that came preinstalled on your computer, as
well as ones you've chosen to install afterward.

# Finding Currently Running Start Screen Apps

By nature, Start screen apps fill the screen.
Switch to another app, and *it* fills the screen,
shoving away the previous app. Because the
Start screen shows only one app at a time, your
other running apps remain hidden beneath an
invisibility cloak.

When you switch to the desktop, you're in yet
another world, away from the land of apps. How do
you return to an app you just used?

To solve that problem, Windows 8 can reveal a list of
your recently used apps, complete with thumbnail
photos, as shown in Figure 4-4. The list conveniently
includes your desktop, letting you shuffle easily
between apps and the desktop.

The thumbnail-filled strip pops up along the screen's
left edge, and it's available whether you're on the
Start screen *or* the desktop.

To see that list of your recently used apps (and to
close unwanted apps, if desired), employ any of these
tricks:

✔ **Mouse:** Point in the screen's top-right corner;
when a thumbnail of your last-used app
appears, slide the mouse down the screen: The
list of your most recently used apps sticks to

the screen's left side. To switch to an app, click it. To close an app, rightclick its thumbnail and choose Close.

✔ **Keyboard:** Press ▊+Tab to see the list of your most recently used apps, as shown in Figure 4-4. While still holding down the ▊ key, press the Tab key; each press of the Tab key highlights a different app on the list. When you've highlighted your desired app, release the ▊ key, and the app fills the screen. (Highlighted an app you want to close? Then press the Del key.)

✔ **Touchscreen:** Slide your finger gently inward from the screen's left edge. When the last-used app begins to appear, slide back toward the left edge; the list of recently used apps sticks to the left edge. Tap any app on the strip to make it fill the screen. To close an unwanted app, drag it off the screen's bottom edge until the app vanishes, like water off a cliff.

**Figure 4-4:** Find recently used apps in a strip along the screen's left edge.

# Chapter 5

# Engaging the Social Apps

*T*hanks to the Internet's never-fading memory, your friends and acquaintances never disappear. Old college chums, business pals, and even those elementary school bullies are all waiting for you online. Toss in a few strangers you may have swapped messages with on websites, and the Internet has created a huge social network.

To manage your online social life, Windows 8 includes a suite of intertwined social apps: Mail, People, Calendar, and Messaging. You can pretty much guess which app handles what job.

The apps work together, vastly simplifying the chore of tracking your contacts and appointments. Tell

Windows 8 about your Facebook account, for example, and Windows 8 automatically stuffs your Facebook friends' information into the People app, adds birthdays and appointments to your Calendar app, and sets up your Mail and Messaging apps.

# *Adding Your Social Accounts to Windows 8*

For years, you've heard people say, "Never tell *anybody* your user account name and password." Now, it seems Windows 8 wants you to break that rule. When you first open your People, Mail, or Messaging app, Windows 8 asks you to enter your account names and passwords from Facebook, Google, Twitter, LinkedIn, Hotmail, and other services.

It's not as scary as you think. Microsoft and the other networks have agreed to share your information, *only if you approve it.* And should you approve it, Windows connects to your social network — Facebook, for example — where you can tell Facebook it's okay to share your information with the People app in Windows 8.

Frankly, approving the information swap is a huge timesaver. When you link those accounts to Windows 8, your computer signs in to each service, imports your friends' contact information, and stocks your apps.

To fill in Windows 8 about your online social life, follow these steps:

1. **From the Start screen, open the Mail app.**

   The tile-filled Start screen, covered in Chapter 1, appears when you first turn on your computer. If it's not onscreen, fetch it with these steps:

- **Mouse:** Point at the top- or bottom-right corner to summon the Charms bar. Then click the Start icon that appears.

- **Keyboard:** Press the ■ key.

- **Touchscreen:** Slide your finger inward from the screen's right edge to fetch the Charms bar and then tap the Start icon.

Click the Mail tile, and the app opens. If you haven't yet signed up for a Microsoft account, you are prompted that you need one. (I explain how to sign up for a Microsoft account in Chapter 1.)

When the Mail app first appears, it usually contains at least one e-mail: a welcome message from Microsoft, shown in Figure 5-1. (Mail also asks you to Allow or Decline the sending of error messages to Microsoft, so the company can improve its products.)

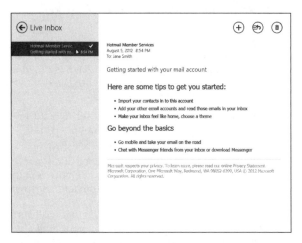

**Figure 5-1:** Add your e-mail accounts from Google, Hotmail, Outlook, and Exchange.

2. **Enter your accounts into the Mail app.**

   To add accounts, summon the Charms bar, click the Settings icon, click Accounts, and click Add an Account. Mail lists the accounts you can add: Hotmail, Outlook, Google, or Exchange.

   To add a Google account, for example, click the word Google. Windows 8 takes you to a secure area on Google's website where you can authorize the transaction by entering your Gmail e-mail address and password and then clicking Connect.

   Repeat these steps for other listed accounts, authorizing each of them to share information with your Windows account.

   I explain how to add e-mail addresses besides Hotmail, Outlook, and Google in the section "Adding other e-mail accounts," later in this chapter.

3. **Return to the Start screen, click the People tile, and enter your other accounts.**

   Now's your chance to tell Windows about your friends: Click the People tile on the Start screen. When it appears, you may spot friends listed in the address books associated with the e-mail accounts you entered in Step 2.

   Continue adding contacts by entering your usernames and passwords from accounts from Facebook, Twitter, LinkedIn, and others.

   For example, choose Facebook, click Connect, and a window appears (shown in Figure 5-2) for you to enter your Facebook name and password.

After you've entered your accounts, Windows 8 automatically fetches your e-mail through your Mail app, fills the People app with your friends' contact information, and adds any appointments in your Calendar app.

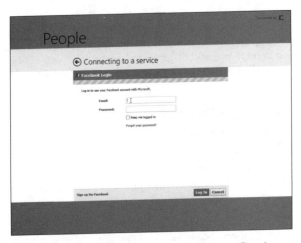

**Figure 5-2:** Import your Facebook friends into your People app.

# Understanding the Mail App

Windows 8 comes with a built-in app for sending and receiving your e-mail. Not only is the Mail app free, but it also comes with a spell checker.

Like many free things, the Mail app carries a cost in convenience, as described by these limitations:

- ✔ You need a Microsoft account to use the Mail app, as well as to use the bundled People, Calendar, and Messaging apps. I describe how to sign up for a free Microsoft account in Chapter 1.

- ✔ The Mail app works only with Hotmail accounts, Windows Live accounts (including Outlook), and Google's Gmail accounts. (It also works with Exchange accounts, but those require special equipment usually found in larger businesses, not homes.)

If you need to add a different type of e-mail account, you do it through Internet Explorer on the Windows desktop. There you can visit your Microsoft or Google account and add other e-mail accounts. I explain how to add another account in the following section.

## Adding other e-mail accounts

The Mail app can fetch e-mail only from Hotmail, Outlook, or Gmail accounts. So, to add other accounts, you need to visit the Windows desktop, open Internet Explorer, and visit www.hotmail.com, www.outlook.com, or Gmail at www.google.com/mail.

From there, open the website's Options menu and look for an area where you can add other accounts. You'll need to enter your account's username and password.

When your Hotmail, Outlook, or Google account begins importing your mail from your other account, that mail will be waiting for you in the Mail app.

## Navigating the Mail app's views, menus, and accounts

To load Windows' Mail app, open the Start screen with a press of your Windows key (⊞) and then click the Mail app tile. The Mail app quickly fills the screen, shown in Figure 5-3.

The Mail app lists your e-mail accounts in its bottom-left corner. Figure 5-3, for example, shows a Hotmail account at the top and a Google account beneath it. (If you've only set up one account, you see only one account listed.)

Mail app folders

Currently viewed e-mail account

Number of unread messages

Latest e-mail from currently viewed account

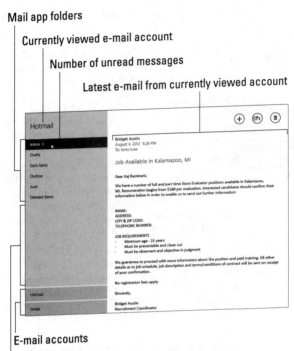

E-mail accounts

Folders on other accounts like Gmail appear here

**Figure 5-3:** The selected e-mail's contents appear on the right.

To see the mail sent to your account, click the account's name. For example, see how the name Hotmail is listed in the top-left corner in Figure 5-3? That's because it's the currently viewed account; accordingly, the Mail app shows the Hotmail account's newest e-mail on the screen's right side.

Beneath the names of your e-mail accounts, the Mail app lists its main folders:

 **Inbox:** Shown when you first load the Mail app, the Inbox folder lists your waiting e-mail. Mail automatically checks for new e-mail, but if you tire of waiting, click Sync, shown in the margin. That immediately grabs any waiting Mail. (Right-click a blank portion of the Mail app to reveal its menus, including the Sync icon along the bottom edge.)

 **Drafts:** When you're midway through writing an e-mail and want to finish it later, click the Close icon shown in the margin and choose Save Draft from the drop-down menu. The e-mail then waits in this folder for retrieval later. (I explain how to send e-mail in this chapter's next section.)

 **Sent Items:** *Every* piece of e-mail you've sent lingers in this folder, leaving a permanent record. (To kill any embarrassing e-mail from any folder, select the offending e-mail with a click and click the Delete icon shown in the margin.)

**Junk:** The Mail app sniffs out potential junk mail and drops suspects into this folder. Peek in here every once in a while to make sure nothing falls in by mistake.

 **Deleted Items:** The Deleted Items folder serves as the Mail app's Recycle Bin, letting you retrieve mistakenly deleted e-mail. To delete something permanently from the Deleted Items folder, select it and choose the Delete icon.

**Outbox:** When you send or reply to a message, the Mail app immediately tries to connect to the Internet and send it. If Mail can't find the Internet, your message lingers here. When you connect to the Internet again, click the Sync button, if necessary, to send it on its way.

To see the contents of any folder, click it. Click any e-mail inside the folder, and its contents appear in the pane to the far right.

Created folders in your Gmail account? When you click your Google account, the Mail app lists those folders beneath the Map app's own folders, as shown in Figure 5-3.

But where are the Mail app's menus? Like *all* Start screen apps, the Mail app hides its menus on an App bar along the screen's bottom edge. You can reveal the App bar in Mail and *any* Windows app with a few tricks.

To summon the App bar along the bottom of any app, choose one of these options:

✔ **Mouse:** Right-click on a blank portion inside the app.

✔ **Keyboard:** Press ⊞+Z.

✔ **Touchscreen:** From the screen's bottom, slide your finger upward.

When the App bar rises from the screen's bottom edge, shown in Figure 5-4, it reveals icons to help you maneuver through the Mail app.

Return to folder view

Currently viewed e-mail account

Delete currently viewed e-mail

Respond to currently viewed e-mail

Create new e-mail

Currently viewed e-mail

Move currently viewed e-mail to a folder

Mark currently viewed e-mail as unread

Pin the current e-mail account as a Start screen tile

Send and receive new messages

App bar

**Figure 5-4:** As in all Start screen apps, the App bar rises from the screen bottom.

## Composing and sending an e-mail

When you're ready to send an e-mail, follow these steps to compose your letter and drop it in the electronic mailbox, sending it through virtual space to the recipient's computer:

1. **From the Start screen, open the Mail app's tile and click the New icon (plus sign) in the program's top-right corner.**

   A New Message window appears, empty and awaiting your words.

   If you've added more than one e-mail account to the Mail app, choose your return address by clicking the downward-pointing arrow in the From box — the box currently listing your e-mail address. Then select the account you want to use for sending that particular mail.

2. **Type your friend's e-mail address into the To box.**

   As you begin typing, the Mail app scans your People app's list for both names and e-mail addresses, listing potential matches below the To box. Spot a match on the list? Click it, and the Mail app automatically fills in the rest of the e-mail address.

   To send an e-mail to several people, click the plus sign to the right of the To box. The People app appears, listing your contacts' names and e-mail addresses. Click the name — or names — of the people you want to receive your e-mail and then click the Add button. The Mail app addresses your e-mail, just as if you'd typed it in manually.

3. **Click in the Subject line and type in a subject.**

   Click the words Add a Subject at the top of the message and type in your own subject. In

Figure 5-5, for example, I've added the subject Memorandum for Success. Although optional, the Subject line helps your friends sort their mail.

4. **Type your message into the large box beneath the Subject line.**

    Type as many words as you want. As you type, the Mail app underlines potentially misspelled words in red. To correct them, right-click the underlined word and choose the correct spelling from the pop-up menu, shown in Figure 5-5.

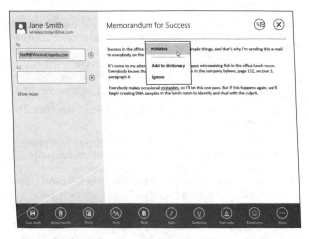

**Figure 5-5:** Type your message, taking advantage of the built-in spell checker.

You can also change formatting by fetching the App bar along the app's bottom edge by right-clicking, by pressing ⊞+Z, or by swiping upward on a tablet. Shown in Figure 5-5, the App bar along the bottom lets you add bulleted lists, change fonts, add italics, and more.

5. **If you want, attach any files or photos to your e-mail.**

   I describe how to attach files in the "Sending and Receiving Files through E-Mail" section, but if you're feeling savvy, you can attach them by clicking the Attachment icon on the Mail app's App bar.

   Most ISPs balk at sending files larger than about 5MB, which rules out nearly all movies and more than a few files containing digital music or photos.

6. **Click the Send button (the envelope) in the top-right corner.**

   Whoosh! The Mail app whisks your message through the Internet to your friend's mailbox. Depending on the speed of your Internet connection, mail can arrive anywhere from 5 seconds later to a few days later, with a few minutes being the average.

   *Don't* want to send the message? Then click the Close button (the X) in the top-right corner. When a drop-down menu appears, choose Delete to delete the message or choose Save Draft to keep a copy in your Drafts folder for later polishing.

## Reading a received e-mail

When your computer is connected to the Internet, the Windows Start screen tells you as soon as a new e-mail arrives. The Mail app's tile automatically updates itself to show the sender and subject of your latest unread e-mails.

To see more information than that — or to respond to the message — follow these steps:

1. **Click the Start screen's Mail tile.**

   Mail opens to show the messages in your Inbox,
   shown earlier in Figure 5-3. Each subject is listed,
   one by one, with the newest one at the top.

   To find a particular e-mail quickly, summon
   the Charms bar's Search pane by pressing
   ⊞+Q and then type the sender's name or a
   keyword in the search box. (You can also
   search for e-mails directly from the Start
   screen's Search pane, covered in Chapter 1.)

2. **Click the subject of any message you want to
   read.**

   The Mail app spills that message's contents into
   the pane along the window's right side.

3. **From here, the Mail app leaves you with several
   options, each accessed from the buttons along
   the e-mail's top edge:**

   - **Nothing:** Undecided? Don't do anything, and
     the message simply sets up camp in your
     Inbox folder.

   - **Respond:** Click the Respond button in the
     top-right corner and choose Reply from the
     drop-down menu. A new window appears,
     ready for you to type in your response. The
     window is just like the one that appears when
     you first compose a message but with a
     handy difference: This window is pre-
     addressed with the recipient's name and the
     subject. Also, the original message usually
     appears at the bottom of your reply for
     reference.

   - **Reply All:** Some people address e-mails to
     several people simultaneously. If you see sev-
     eral other people listed on an e-mail's To line,
     you can reply to all of them by clicking

Respond and choosing Reply All from the drop-down menu.

• **Forward:** Received something that a friend simply must see? Click Respond and choose Forward from the drop-down menu to kick a copy of the e-mail to your friend's Inbox.

• **Delete:** Click the Delete button to toss the message into your Deleted Items folder. Your deleted messages sit inside that folder until you open the Deleted Items folder, click all the messages, and click the Delete button again.

To print your currently viewed e-mail, summon the Charms bar, click the Devices icon, choose your printer from the list of devices, and click the Print button.

# Sending and Receiving Files through E-Mail

Like a pair of movie tickets slipped into the envelope of a thank-you note, an *attachment* is a file that piggy-backs onto an e-mail message. You can send or receive any type of file as an attachment.

This section describes how to both send and receive a file through the Mail app.

## Saving a received attachment

When an attachment arrives in an e-mail, you'll recognize it: It's a large rectangle at the top of your e-mail; the rectangle lists the file's name with the word Download listed directly beneath it.

Saving the attached file or files takes just a few steps.

1. **Click the word Download next to the attached file.**

   This tells the Mail app to actually download the file. Until you click the rectangle, the Mail app tells you only the attached file's name and file size. When the download completes, the rectangle turns into an icon representing the newly downloaded file.

2. **When the file downloads to the Mail app, click the attached file's icon and choose Save.**

   That tells the Mail app to copy the file from your e-mail and save it to a folder in your computer.

3. **Choose a folder to receive the saved file.**

   The Windows 8 File Picker appears, shown in Figure 5-6, letting you navigate to a folder.

**Figure 5-6:** To save an attached file, choose Files, choose a location to save the file, and then click the Save button.

4. **Click the word Files in the File Picker's top-left corner and then choose which library to receive the incoming file: Documents, Pictures, Music, or Videos.**

   Saving the file inside one of your four libraries is the easiest way to ensure you'll find it later.

5. **Click the Save button in the File Picker's bottom-right corner.**

   The Mail app saves the file in the library of your choosing.

After you've saved the file, the Mail app returns to the screen. And, if you notice, the attachment still remains inside the e-mail. That's because saving attachments always saves a *copy* of the sent file. That's handy because, if you accidentally delete your saved file, you can return to the original e-mail and save the file yet again.

The built-in virus checker in Windows 8, Windows Defender, automatically scans your incoming e-mail for any evil file attachments.

## Sending a file as an attachment

Sending a file through the Mail app works much like saving an attached file, although in reverse: Instead of grabbing a file from an e-mail and saving it into a folder or library, you're grabbing a file from a folder or library and saving it in an e-mail.

To send a file as an attachment in the Mail app, follow these steps:

1. **Open the Mail app and click the plus sign to create a new e-mail, as described earlier in this chapter's "Composing and sending an e-mail" section.**

2. **Open the Mail app's App bar and click the Attachments (paper clip) icon.**

   Open the App bar by right-clicking a blank part of the e-mail. When you click the Attachments icon, the Windows 8 File Picker window appears, shown earlier in Figure 5-6.

3. **Navigate to the file you'd like to send.**

   For easy browsing, click the word Files. That fetches a drop-down menu, shown earlier in Figure 5-6, listing your computer's major storage areas. Most files are stored in your Documents, Pictures, Music and Videos libraries.

    Click a folder's name to see the files it contains. Not the right folder? Click the File Picker's Go Up link to move back out of the folder and try again.

4. **Click the filenames you want to send and click the Attach button.**

   Selected too many files? Deselect unwanted files by clicking their names yet again. When you click the Attach button, the Mail app adds the file or files to your e-mail.

5. **Click the Send button (the envelope icon).**

   The Mail app whisks off your mail and its attachment to the recipient.

## Finding lost mail

Eventually, an important e-mail will disappear into a pile of folders and filenames. To retrieve it, rely on the same trick you use to search within *any* app in Windows 8: Summon the Search pane. From within Windows Mail, click the account holding the e-mail you want to search through and then follow these steps:

> ✔ **Mouse:** Point in the screen's top- or bottom-right corners; when the Charms bar appears, click the Search icon.
>
> ✔ **Keyboard:** Press +Q.
>
> ✔ **Touchscreen:** Slide your finger inward from the screen's right edge and tap the Search icon.

When the Search pane appears, type in a word or the person's name and then press Enter to see all your matching e-mail.

> **REMEMBER**
>
> If you have more than one account in Mail, you must search each account separately.

## Managing Your Contacts in the People App

 When you let Windows 8 eavesdrop on your online social networks, as described in this chapter's first section, you've conveniently stocked the People app with your online friends from Facebook, Twitter, and other networks.

To see everybody in your People app, click the Start screen's People tile. The People app appears, listing all your online friends, as shown in Figure 5-7.

The People app handles much of its upkeep automatically, axing people you've unfriended on Facebook, for example, and slyly removing contacts who've unfriended *you*, as well.

But friends who don't share their lives online through social networks won't appear in the People app. And some privacy-concerned Facebook friends may have told Facebook to withhold their information from other programs — and that includes Windows 8.

**Figure 5-7:** The People app stocks itself with friends from your social networks.

That means you'll need to edit some People entries manually. This section explains the occasional pruning needed to keep up with our constantly evolving social networks.

## Adding contacts

Although the People app loves to reach its fingers into any online crevice you toss its way, you can easily add people the old-fashioned way, typing them in by hand.

To add somebody to the People app, which makes those names available in your Mail and Messaging apps, follow these steps:

1. **Click the People tile on the Start screen.**

2. **Right-click on a blank part of the People app, and the App bar rises from the program's bottom edge. Then click the New icon.**

   A blank New Contact form makes its appearance.

3. **Fill out the New Contact form.**

   Shown in Figure 5-8, most of the choices are self-explanatory fields such as Name, Address, Email, and Phone. Click the Other Info button on the right to add items such as a job title, website, significant other, or notes.

**Figure 5-8:** Add information about your new contact. Then click Save.

   The biggest challenge comes with the Account field, an option seen only by people who've entered more than one e-mail account into the Mail app. Which e-mail *account* should receive the new contact?

The answer hinges mainly on which cellphone you own. Choose your Google account if you use an Android phone, so your newly added account will appear on your Android phone's contacts list.

Choose the Microsoft account if you use a Microsoft phone, so the contact will appear there.

**4. Click the Save button.**

The People app dutifully saves your new contact. If you spot a mistake, however, you may need to go back and edit the information, described in the next section.

## Deleting or editing contacts

Has somebody fallen from your social graces? Or perhaps just changed a phone number? Either way, it's easy to delete or edit a contact by following these steps:

**1. Click the People tile on the Start screen.**

The People app appears, as shown earlier in Figure 5-7.

**2. Click a contact.**

The contact's page appears full-screen.

**3. Right-click a blank part of the contact's page to summon the App bar.**

The App bar appears as a strip along the screen's bottom.

**4. Click Delete to delete the contact or click Edit to update a contact's information. Then click Save.**

Clicking Delete removes the person completely. However, the Delete button appears only for contacts you've added *by hand*. If they've been added through Facebook or another online social media site, you have to delete them by removing them from your contacts on that site. Unfriend them on Facebook or unfollow them on Twitter, for example, to remove them from the People app.

Clicking Edit fetches the screen shown back in Figure 5-8, where you can update or delete any information before clicking Save to save your changes.

Designed for best friends, the Pin to Start button turns that person into a Start screen tile, giving you easy access to her contact information and latest status updates.

To send a quick message to a contact in your People app, click her name. When her contact information appears, click the Send Email button. The Mail app calls up a handy, pre-addressed New Message window, ready for you to type your message and click Send. (This trick works only if you have that contact's e-mail address.)

# Managing Appointments in Calendar

After you enter your social networking accounts such as Facebook and Google, as described in this chapter's first section, you've already stocked the Calendar app with appointments entered by both you and your online friends.

The Calendar displays your Facebook friends' birthdays, for example — if your Facebook friends have chosen to share that information. You can also find any appointments you've made in Google's calendar, a handy perk for owners of Android phones.

To see your appointments, click the Start screen's Calendar tile. The Calendar app appears, listing all your online appointments, as shown in Figure 5-9.

**Figure 5-9:** The Calendar app gets appointments from your online social networks.

Very few people keep all their appointments online, though, so you'll occasionally need to edit some entries, add new ones, or delete those you can no longer attend. This section explains how to keep your appointments up-to-date.

The Calendar opens to show a monthly view, shown earlier in Figure 5-9. To switch to other views, right-click the Calendar app to fetch the App bar; then click the Day, Week, or Month button.

 No matter which view the Calendar app displays, you can flip through the appointments by clicking the little arrows near the screen's top corners. Click the right arrow to move forward in time; click the left arrow to move backward.

The Calendar app grabs whatever appointments it can find from your online social networks. But you can still add or edit appointments manually when needed.

To add an appointment to your Calendar app, follow these steps:

1. **Click the Calendar tile on the Start screen.**

   The Calendar appears, shown earlier in Figure 5-9.

2. **Load the Apps bar and click the New icon.**

   I explain how to load any app's menu bar earlier in this chapter. (*Hint:* Right-click anywhere on the Calendar.)

3. **Fill out the Details form.**

   Shown in Figure 5-10, most of the choices are self-explanatory fields.

   The biggest challenge comes with the Calendar field, an option available only if you've entered more than one e-mail account into your Mail app. Which e-mail *account* should receive the new calendar appointment?

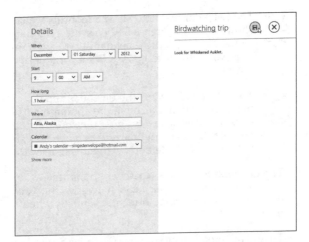

**Figure 5-10:** Add your appointment's date, start time, duration, and other details.

# Chatting through Messaging

A computing staple for decades, instant messaging apps let you exchange messages with other online friends. Unlike e-mail, instant messaging takes place, well, *instantly*. The screen displays two boxes, and you type messages back and forth to each other.

Messaging apps spawn a love/hate relationship. Some people love the convenience and intimacy of keeping in touch with faraway friends. Others hate feeling trapped in an elevator and forced to make small talk.

But love it or hate it, the Windows Messaging app handles both heartfelt conversations and idle chatter. And even if your online friends use different messaging services and programs, Windows Messaging can swap messages with them all.

To begin swapping small talk, er, philosophical conversations with your online friends, follow these steps:

1. **From the Start screen, click the Messaging tile.**

   The Messaging app appears, shown in Figure 5-11.

**Figure 5-11:** The Messaging app lists previous conversations on the left edge; click a conversation to see its contents on the right.

2. **Click the New Message link.**

   Shown in the top-left corner of Figure 5-11, the New Message link lets you see which of your friends are currently online in their own messaging programs. If a friend doesn't appear here, she's either not online, or she's not listed in your People app.

3. **Click the person you'd like to chat with.**

   When the messaging window appears, begin typing, as shown in Figure 5-12. Your friend will see a notice from his or her own messaging program, whether it's on Facebook, a cellphone, or a different system.

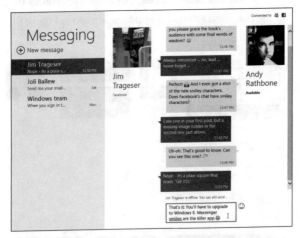

**Figure 5-12:** Press Enter to send your message to your friend.

When you press Enter, your message appears in your friend's messaging program. And that's it. When you're done typing messages to each other, just say goodbye. The next time you visit the Messaging app, your conversation will still be there, waiting to be continued, if you wish.

To delete a conversation, right-click inside the Messaging app to fetch the App bar and then click the Delete icon, shown in the margin.

# Chapter 6

# Getting Connected and Having Fun through the Start Screen

. . . . . . . . . . . . . . . . . . . . . . . . . . . . . .

## In This Chapter

▶ Connecting to the web wirelessly

▶ Playing music from the Start screen

▶ Taking photos with your computer's camera

▶ Viewing photos in your Pictures library

. . . . . . . . . . . . . . . . . . . . . . . . . . . . . .

*1*n this chapter, you find out how to connect to the Internet so you can visit websites and find all the good stuff online that you can access from the Start screen.

Then, you check out the Windows 8 Media Player that's bound to the Start screen and find out how to get the most from it.

Finally, this chapter shows you how to take pictures with the Start screen's Camera App (using the digital camera that's built into your computer), as well as how to view and share your photos.

# Why Do I Need an ISP?

Everybody needs three things to connect with the Internet: a computer, web browser software, and an *Internet service provider* (ISP).

You already have the computer, be it a tablet, laptop, or desktop PC. And Windows 8 comes with a pair of web browsers. The Start screen's Internet Explorer browser works for full-screen, quick information grabs; the desktop's Internet Explorer browser offers more in-depth features.

Most people only need to find an ISP. Ask your friends and neighbors how they connect and whether they recommend their ISP. Call several ISPs serving your area for a rate quote and then compare rates. Most bill on a monthly basis, so if you're not happy, you can always switch.

ISPs let you connect to the Internet in a variety of ways. The slowest ISPs require a dialup modem and an ordinary phone line. Faster still are *broadband* connections: special DSL or ISDN lines provided by some phone companies, and the even faster cable modems, supplied by your cable television company. When shopping for broadband ISPs, your geographic location usually determines your options.

 You need to pay an ISP for only *one* Internet connection. By setting up a network, you can share that single connection with any other computers, cellphones, TVs, and other Internet-aware gadgetry in your home or office.

# *Connecting Wirelessly to the Internet*

Windows *constantly* searches for a working Internet connection. If it finds one that you've used previously, you're set: Windows passes the news along to Internet Explorer, and you're ready to visit the web.

When you're traveling, however, the wireless networks around you will often be new, so you'll have to authorize these new connections.

To connect to a nearby wireless network for the first time, either one in your own home or in a public place, follow these steps:

1. **Summon the Charms bar and click or tap the Settings icon.**

   Any of these three tricks summons the Charms bar and its Settings screen:

   • **Mouse:** Point at the screen's top- or bottom-right edge; when the Charms bar appears, click the Settings icon.

   • **Keyboard:** Press ⊞+I to head straight for the Charms bar's Settings screen.

   • **Touchscreen:** Slide your finger inward from the screen's right edge; when the Charms bar appears, tap the Settings icon.

2. **Click or tap the wireless network icon.**

   Among the Settings screen's six icons, the one in the top left represents wireless networks. The icon changes shape, depending on your surroundings:

- **Available:** When the icon says Available, you're within range of a wireless network. Start salivating and move to the next step.

- **Unavailable:** When the icon says Unavailable, you're out of range. Time to head for a different seat in the coffee shop or perhaps a different coffee shop altogether. Then return to Step 1.

3. **Click or tap the Available icon if it's present.**

   Windows lists all the wireless networks within range of your PC. Don't be surprised to see several networks listed; if you're at home, your neighbors probably see your network listed, too.

4. **Choose to connect to the desired network by clicking its name and clicking the Connect button.**

    If you select the adjacent Connect Automatically check box before clicking the Connect button, Windows automatically connects to that network the next time you're within range, sparing you from connecting manually each time.

   If you're connecting to an *unsecured network* — a network that doesn't require a password — you're finished. Windows warns you about connecting to an unsecured network, but a click or tap of the Connect button lets you connect anyway. (Don't do any shopping or banking on an unsecured connection.)

5. **Enter a password if needed.**

   If you try to connect to a *security-enabled* wireless connection, Windows asks you to enter a *network security key* — technospeak for *password.* If you're at home, here's where you type in the same password you entered into your router when you set up your wireless network.

If you're connecting to somebody *else's* password-protected wireless network, ask the network's owner for the password. If you're in a hotel, pull out your credit card. You probably need to buy some connection time from the people behind the front desk.

6. **Choose whether you want to share your files with other people on the network.**

    If you're connecting on your own home or office network, choose "Yes, turn on sharing and connect to devices." That lets you share files with others and use handy devices, like printers.

    If you're connecting in a public area, by contrast, choose "No, don't turn on sharing or connect to devices." That keeps out snoops.

 If you're still having problems connecting, try the following tips:

✔ When Windows says that it can't connect to your wireless network, it offers to bring up the Network Troubleshooter. The Network Troubleshooter mulls over the problem and then says something about the signal being weak. It's really telling you this: "Move closer to the wireless transmitter."

✔ If you can't connect to the secured network you want, try connecting to one of the unsecured networks. Unsecured networks work fine for casual browsing on the Internet.

✔ Cordless phones and microwave ovens, oddly enough, interfere with wireless networks. Try to keep your cordless phone out of the same room as your wireless PC, and don't heat up that sandwich when web browsing.

 If your desktop's taskbar contains a wireless network icon (shown in the margin), click it to jump to Step 3. While you're working on the Windows 8 desktop, that wireless network icon provides a handy way to connect wirelessly in new locations.

# Browsing Quickly from the Start Screen

 To open the Internet Explorer app from the Start screen, click its tile, shown in the margin. The browser opens, filling the screen with your last-viewed site.

When you want to visit someplace else, fetch the browser's hidden menus with any of these commands:

- ✔ **Mouse:** Right-click a blank portion of the web page, away from any words or pictures.
- ✔ **Keyboard:** Press ⊞+Z.
- ✔ **Touchscreen:** From the screen's top or bottom edge, slide your finger toward the screen's center.

The browser's top and bottom menus are neatly labeled in Figure 6-1.

New InPrivate window/Close tabs

Currently open websites          Open new blank tab

Address Bar          Reload web page

Revisit previous web page          Pin to Start screen

Search page/View on desktop browser

Currently viewed web page   Move forward one web page

**Figure 6-1:** The Start screen's browser offers hidden menus along the top and bottom.

# Playing Music from the Start Screen

The Start screen's Music app isn't as much of a music player as it is an online storefront. Shown in Figure 6-2, the program devotes most of its onscreen real estate to advertising: Billboard-like tiles promote the latest releases by the latest artists.

**Figure 6-2:** The Start screen's music player resembles a store-front more than a music player.

And your *own* music? Scroll to the left, and you'll find tiles dedicated to music already on your computer. To launch the Music app and begin playing (or buying) music, follow these steps:

1. **Click the Start screen's Music tile.**

   The Start screen appears when you first turn on your computer. To find it from the desktop, press the Windows key () or point your mouse cursor to the bottom-left corner and click.

   On a touchscreen, slide your finger inward from any screen's right edge to summon the Charms bar; then tap the Start icon to return to the Start screen.

2. **Sign in with your Microsoft account or your Xbox Live account, if desired, or click Cancel.**

   Each time you open the Music app, Microsoft tries to link the Music app with your Microsoft account or Xbox Live account. Because those accounts can be linked to a credit card, you need one of those accounts to buy music.

3. **Scroll to the right to sample or buy new music.**

   The Music app, shown earlier in Figure 6-2, contains several screens, which you navigate by pressing the right-arrow key or pointing your mouse to the screen's right or left edge.

   The opening screen shows either pictures of popular artists or a collage of the music stored on your computer. In the bottom-left corner, shown earlier in Figure 6-2, the opening screen lists the last song you heard. Click the Play button to hear it again.

   The second screen to the right, called Xbox Music Store, lets you listen to song previews from the latest CDs and purchase the songs if you like. One more screen to the right reveals Most Popular, yet another storefront for the latest popular tunes.

4. **Scroll to the far left to see and play music stored on your computer.**

   To head straight for your own music, scroll to the far left; there, the My Music screen lists music stored on your own computer. Click an album's tile to see its songs.

   To see *all* your stored music, click the words My Music at the screen's top; a list of your music appears, letting you sort it alphabetically by songs, albums, artists, or playlists.

5. **To play an album or song, click its tile and then click Play.**

   Click a tile for an album or song, and the mini-player finally appears. Depending on the licensing agreements and your own equipment, you can choose to play it on your computer, play it on your Xbox, or add it to a playlist.

6. **Adjust the music while it plays.**

   Right-click the screen (or tap it with a touch-screen) to bring up the controls on the App bar, shown in Figure 6-3. The App bar offers you five icons to control your music: Shuffle, Repeat, Previous (to move to the previous song), Pause, and Next (to move to the next song).

   As the music plays, the Music app shows a collage of your music's cover art, but it tosses in art from other artists in the hopes that it will inspire an impulse purchase.

 To adjust the volume, summon the Charms bar by pressing ■+C or pointing your mouse cursor at the screen's bottom-right corner. Click the Settings icon, click the Sound icon, and slide the volume indicator up or down.

**Figure 6-3:** While music plays, right-click the screen to bring up the controls for shuffling, pausing, and moving between tracks.

# *Taking Photos with the Camera App*

Most tablets, laptops, and some desktop computers come with built-in cameras, sometimes called *webcams*. Their tiny cameras can't take high-resolution close-ups of that rare bird in the neighbor's tree, but they work fine for their main purpose: Taking a quick photo to e-mail to friends or post on Facebook.

To take a photo through your computer's camera with the Camera app, follow these steps:

1. **From the Start screen, click the Camera tile to open the app.**

2. **If the app asks to use your camera and microphone, choose Allow.**

   As a security precaution, Windows asks permission to turn on your camera. That helps prevent sneaky apps from spying on you without your knowing.

   After you grant approval, the computer screen turns into a giant viewfinder, showing you exactly what the camera sees: your face.

3. **Adjust the settings, if desired.**

   Depending on your type of camera, the Camera's App bar offers different icons, as shown in Figure 6-4:

   - **Change camera:** Meant for laptops and tablets with front- and back-facing cameras, this button lets you toggle between the two.

   - **Camera Options:** Clicking this icon brings the pop-up menu similar to the one shown in the right of Figure 6-4. Here, you can choose your camera's resolution and toggle between different microphones attached to your computer. If you see More Options at the pop-up menu's bottom edge, choose it to tweak even more options offered by your particular camera.

- **Timer:** Helpful for setting up shots, this tells the camera to snap the photo three seconds *after* you click the screen. (When you click the icon, it turns white, letting you know it's turned on.)

- **Video mode:** Click this icon to shoot videos rather than still shots. Clicking the screen toggles the video on and off. (The video icon turns white when activated, so you know the camera's in video mode.) While recording, a small timer appears in the screen's bottom-right corner, letting you know the video's current length.

**Figure 6-4:** Choose your camera's options and then click anywhere on the screen to snap a photo or video.

4. **To snap a photo, click anywhere on the screen.**

   To see the photo you just snapped, click the arrow on the left edge of the screen; to return to the Camera app, click the arrow to the right of the screen.

> The Camera app saves all your snapped photos and videos in a folder called Camera Roll in your Pictures library.

# Viewing Photos from the Start Screen

The two-headed beast of Windows 8 naturally includes *two* ways to view your digital photos on your computer: the Start screen's Photos app and the Desktop app's Photo Viewer.

The Start screen's Photos app works best for quickly showing off photos. It pulls in photos from your social networks such as Facebook and Flickr, making it easy to display *all* your photos from within one program.

What the Photos app lacks, however, are options. It won't rotate a sideways photo so it's right-side-up. You can't see the date you snapped a photo, or which camera snapped it. It's awkward for managing photos. It can't print, nor can it crop.

But when you want to show off your photos without a lot of fuss, follow these steps:

1. **From the Start screen, click the Photos tile.**

   The Photos app quickly appears, shown in Figure 6-5, showing tiles representing your main photo storage areas:

- **Pictures Library:** These photos live in your *own* computer, inside your Pictures library. You can see these photos even if you're not connected to the Internet. Photos stored in the other areas, by contrast, can't usually be seen without an Internet connection.

- **SkyDrive:** These photos live on Microsoft's huge Internet-connected computers. You can access them from any Internet-connected computer after you enter your Microsoft account and password. (I cover Microsoft accounts in Chapter 1, and SkyDrive in Chapter 3.)

- **Facebook:** This area shows all the photos you've uploaded to your Facebook account (www.facebook.com).

- **Flickr:** These photos come from your account on Flickr (www.flickr.com), one of many photo-sharing sites.

**Figure 6-5:** The Start screen's Photos app lists your photo storage areas.

2. **Click a storage area to see its photos; while inside any storage area, right-click the screen to see its App bar, which offers that screen's particular menus.**

   Click or tap a storage area to see the photos and folders hidden inside. The Photos app shows photos in a long horizontal strip across your screen, as shown in Figure 6-6. The folder's name appears across the top.

Return to previous folder

Name of current folder

Location of current folder

Number of files in current folder

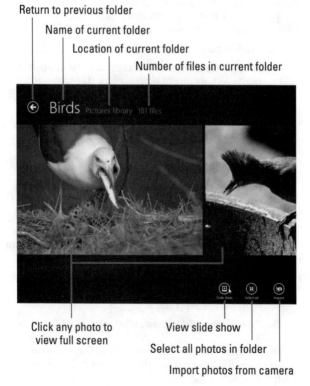

Click any photo to view full screen

View slide show

Select all photos in folder

Import photos from camera

**Figure 6-6:** Scroll to the left or right to see the photos.

On a touchscreen, slide your finger up from the screen's bottom edge to see the App bar. Depending on what you're viewing, you'll see icons to Delete, Select All, Browse by Date, or see a Slide Show.

To navigate between folders, click the left-pointing arrow in the screen's top-left corner. (Click or tap the photo to bring a missing arrow into view.)

To delete a photo, right-click it and then click the Delete icon (shown in the margin) from the App bar along the screen's bottom edge.

3. **Click a photo to see it full-screen.**

   When a photo fills the screen, an arrow appears on its left and right edges; click the arrow to move from photo to photo.

   On a touchscreen, tap a photo to view it full-screen, and then tap the side arrows to navigate between photos.

   Viewing a photo that a friend *has* to see? E-mail it to her. I describe the details in Chapter 5, but here's the quick-and-dirty version: Fetch the Charms bar, click the Share icon (or press ⊞+H), and click Mail.

   To return to the strip view of your photos, click the left-pointing arrow at the top-left corner. (You may need to click the photo to see the arrow.)

4. **To view a slide show of the current folder, right-click any photo and then click the Slide Show icon on the App bar.**

5. **To exit the slide show, click any photo.**

To exit the Photos app, head for the Start screen: Press the ⊞ key or fetch the Charms bar and click the Start icon.

# Chapter 7

# Ten Things You'll Hate about Windows 8 (And How to Fix Them)

*H*ere are some of the most aggravating things about Windows 8 — and how to fix them.

## 1 Want to Avoid the Start Screen!

No matter how many Start screen–avoiding tactics you may employ, you'll still find yourself tossed back onto the Start screen when you do any of the following things:

✔ **Add user accounts.** The desktop's Control Panel lets you manage a user account. You can toggle a user account between Standard and Administrator, change its name, and even delete it completely. But if you need to *add* a user account — or even change your own account's picture — you're dropped off at the Start screen's PC Settings screen to finish the job.

✔ **Play a music file or view a photo.** Windows 8 sets itself up to use the Start screen's Music and Photos apps. Open one photo or MP3 file on the desktop, and you'll find yourself back in Start screen land.

✔ **Troubleshoot.** Although the Start screen specializes in rather anemic faire, it also contains two of the most powerful troubleshooting tools in Windows 8: Refresh and Remove Everything. These two tools offer last-ditch cure-alls for ailing computers. You won't find any way to access these tools from the desktop, however.

In short, be prepared for the occasional unavoidable journey to the Start screen.

# *I Want to Avoid the Desktop!*

On a touchscreen tablet, it's enticing to stay on the Start screen with its finger-sized tiles and easy-to-touch icons. Smartphone owners have enjoyed the app lifestyle for years.

But staying nestled within the Start screen's world of apps can be more difficult than it appears. No matter how hard you try to avoid the desktop and its pin-sized controls, you'll find yourself dragged there when you do any of the following things from the Start screen:

✔ **Click the Desktop tile.** This app brings you straight to the desktop zone. To hide this tile or any other Start screen tile, right-click the unwanted app to reveal the App bar and then click the Unpin from Start icon.

✔ **Browse files.** The Start screen isn't sophisticated enough to browse your files. As soon as you plug in a flash drive or portable hard drive, the desktop's File Explorer leaps onscreen to handle the job.

✔ **Manage a user account.** You can *create* new accounts from the Start screen, but to *delete* or *change* an existing account, you need the desktop's Control Panel.

✔ **Watch Flash videos.** The Start screen's version of Internet Explorer handles most websites well. But on some websites, it can't play videos that employ Adobe Flash technology. When a video won't play, right-click a blank part of the website to reveal the App bar. Then click the Page Tool icon (wrench inside a circle), and choose View on the Desktop. The desktop's Internet Explorer jumps in to finish the task.

✔ **Manage gadgetry.** The Start screen's PC Settings screen lists all the devices connected to your computer, from printers to mice to portable hard drives. But it shows only their names; to change the *settings* of any of those devices requires a trip to the desktop's Control Panel.

✔ **Manage files.** You can access your photos and music files from the Start screen's Photos and Music apps, respectively. But *changing* those files in any way — renaming a file or folder, perhaps — requires a trip to the desktop. You'll find yourself there when looking for the date you snapped a photo, as well.

In short, the Start screen works well for most simple computing tasks. But when it comes to fine-tuning your computer's settings, performing maintenance work, or even browsing files, you'll find yourself returning to the desktop.

# *1 Can't Copy Music to My iPod*

You won't find the word *iPod* mentioned in the Windows 8 menus, help screens, or even in the Help areas of Microsoft's website. That's because Microsoft's competitor, Apple, makes the tremendously popular iPod. Microsoft's strategy is to ignore the little gizmo in the hope that it will go away.

What won't go away, though, are the problems you'll face if you ever try to copy songs onto an iPod with Media Player. You face two hurdles:

- ✔ Windows Media Player won't recognize your iPod, much less send it any songs or videos.

- ✔ When you plug in your iPod, Windows might recognize the slick gadget as a portable hard drive. It may even let you copy songs to it. But your iPod won't be able to find or play them.

The easiest solution is to download and install iTunes software from Apple's website (www.apple.com/itunes). Because iTunes and Media Player will bicker over which program can play your files, you'll probably end up choosing iTunes.

# *1 Always Have to Sign In*

The power-conscious Windows 8 normally blanks your screen when you haven't touched a key for a few minutes. And, when you belatedly press a key to bring the screen back to life, you're faced with the lock screen.

To move past the lock screen, you need to type your password to sign back in to your account.

Some people prefer that extra level of security. If the lock screen kicks in while you're spending too much time at the water cooler, you're protected: Nobody can walk over and snoop through your e-mail. Other people don't need that extra security, and they simply want to return to work quickly.

If you don't *ever* want to see the lock screen, use a single user account without a password. That defeats all the security offered by the user account system, but it's more convenient if you live alone.

To keep Windows from asking for a password whenever it wakes back up, follow these steps:

1. **Right-click in any screen's bottom-left corner and then choose Control Panel.**

2. **From the Control Panel, click System and Security and then click Power Options.**

3. **From the screen's left edge, click Require a Password on Wakeup.**

   When the window appears, most of the options are *grayed out* — inaccessible.

4. **Select the option labeled Change Settings That Are Currently Unavailable.**

5. **Select the Don't Require a Password option and then click the Save Changes button.**

That leaves you with a more easy-going Windows.
When your computer wakes up from sleep, you're left
at the same place where you stopped working, and
you don't have to enter your password anymore.

Unfortunately, it also leaves you with a less-secure
Windows. Anybody who walks by your computer will
have access to all your files.

To return to the safer-but-less-friendly Windows,
follow these same steps, but in Step 5, select the
Require a Password (Recommended) option. Then
click the Save Changes button.

# The Taskbar Keeps Disappearing

If your taskbar suddenly clings to the *side* of the
screen instead of where it usually squats along the
bottom of the desktop, try dragging it back in place:
Instead of dragging an edge, drag the entire taskbar
from its middle. As your mouse pointer reaches your
desktop's bottom edge, the taskbar suddenly snaps
back into place. Let go of the mouse, and you've
recaptured it.

Follow these tips to prevent your taskbar from
wandering:

- ✔ To keep the taskbar locked into place so that
  it won't float away, right-click a blank part of
  the taskbar and select Lock the Taskbar.
  Remember, though, that before you can make
  any future changes to the taskbar, you must
  first unlock it.

- ✔ If your taskbar drops from sight whenever the
  mouse pointer doesn't hover nearby, turn off
  the taskbar's Auto Hide feature: Right-click a

blank part of the taskbar and choose Properties from the pop-up menu. When the Taskbar Properties dialog box appears, deselect the Auto-Hide the Taskbar check box. (Or, to turn on the Auto Hide feature, select the check box.)

# I Can't Keep Track of Open Windows

You don't *have* to keep track of all those open windows. Windows 8 does it for you with a secret key combination: Hold the Alt key and press the Tab key, and a little bar appears, displaying the icons for all your open windows. Keep pressing Tab; when Windows highlights the icon of the window you're after, release the keys. The window pops up.

Or visit the taskbar, that long strip along the bottom of your screen. Mentioned in Chapter 2, the taskbar lists the name of every open window. Click the name of the window you want, and that window hops to the top of the pile.

If a program icon on the taskbar contains several open windows — you're simultaneously editing several documents in Microsoft Word, for example — right-click the Microsoft Word icon. A pop-up menu appears, letting you click the document you want to access.

Can't find a previously opened Start screen app? Hold down the ▓ key and press the Tab key: Thumbnail images of all your open apps appear on a strip along the screen's left edge. Keep pressing the Tab key until you've highlighted the desired app; let go of the Tab key, and the selected app fills the screen.

# I Can't Line Up Two Windows on the Screen

With its arsenal of dragging-and-dropping tools, Windows simplifies grabbing information from one window and copying it to another. You can drag an address from an address book and drop it atop a letter in your word processor, for example.

However, the hardest part of dragging and dropping comes when you're lining up two windows on the screen, side by side, for dragging.

Windows 8 offers an easy way to align windows for easy dragging and dropping:

1. **Drag one window against a left or right edge.**

   When your mouse pointer touches the screen's edge, the window reshapes itself to fill half the screen.

2. **Drag the other window against the opposite edge.**

   When your mouse pointer reaches the opposite edge, the two windows are aligned side by side.

You can also minimize all the windows except for the two you want to align side by side. Then right-click a blank spot on the taskbar, and then choose Show Windows Side By Side. The two windows line up on the screen perfectly.

# It Won't Let Me Do Something Unless I'm an Administrator!

Windows 8 gets really picky about who gets to do what on your computer. The computer's owner gets the Administrator account. And the administrator usually gives everybody else a Standard account. What does that mean? Well, only the administrator can do the following things on the computer:

- ✔ Install programs and hardware.
- ✔ Create or change accounts for other people.
- ✔ Start an Internet connection.
- ✔ Install some hardware, such as digital cameras and MP3 players.
- ✔ Perform actions affecting other people on the PC.

People with Standard accounts, by nature, are limited to fairly basic activities. They can do these things:

- ✔ Run previously installed programs.
- ✔ Change their account's picture and password.

Guest accounts are meant for the babysitter or visitors who don't permanently use the computer. If you have a broadband or other "always on" Internet account, guests can browse the Internet, run programs, or check their e-mail. (Guest accounts aren't allowed to *start* an Internet session, but they can use an existing one.)

If Windows says only an administrator may do something on your PC, you have two choices: Find an administrator to type his or her password and authorize the action; or convince an administrator to upgrade your account to an Administrator account.

# I Don't Know What Version of Windows I Have

To find out what version of Windows is installed on your computer, right-click in the bottom-left corner of any screen. When the pop-up menu appears, choose System. When the System window appears, look near the top to see which version of Windows 8 you own: Windows 8 (for consumers), Windows Pro (for small businesses), Enterprise (for large businesses), or Windows RT.

# My Print Screen Key Doesn't Work

Contrary to its name, the Print Screen key doesn't shuttle a picture of your screen to your printer. Instead, the Print Screen key (usually labeled PrintScreen, PrtScr, or PrtSc) sends the screen's picture to the Windows 8 memory. From there, you can paste it into a graphics program, such as Paint, letting the graphics program send the picture to the printer.

 Windows 8 introduces something new, though: If you want to capture an image of the entire screen and save it as a file, press ⊞+PrtScr.

That tells Windows to snap a picture of your current screen and save it in your Pictures library with the name *Screenshot.* (Windows saves those images in the PNG format, if you're interested, and it captures your mouse pointer, as well.) Subsequent screenshots include a number after the name, like Screenshot (2) and Screenshot (3).

When saved, your screenshot can head for your printer when you right-click the file and choose Print from the pop-up menu.